I'm called a survivor, but not of my choosing. My son killed himself, and the gut-wrenching pain rained down on me like a gulley-washer. There was no surviving without help, which came in the form of a still, small voice telling me to write to Him about my feelings. Through this simple beginning poured forth words that lined up in an amazing journey carrying me through the tunnel of suffering and into the sunshine of God's Love.

Dedicated to my husband and children
who have had to shoulder their own burdens of grief
as we travel this road together.

ENDORSEMENTS

"The sure and certain hope of the future is clearly seen in the deeply personal journey of this shared experience. It not only lifts the darkness of utter despair and pain in losing a loved one in an unnatural way but brings with it a clear and decisive peace that transcends the here and now and reaches forward to the sure certainty of tomorrow. I believe when you have finished walking through these pages your heart will be lifted up and encouraged."

Esmé Ross-Pastoral Team Ministry

"*Shattered By Suicide* is a conversation between a grieving mother and her Heavenly Father, and His answers are shared from His Word, the Bible. Have you ever wondered what to say to a grieving family of a suicide victim? This book helped me understand the family's point of view. I admire Gracie for sharing such a personal time of her life to help others with the many unanswered questions we have on the subject of suicide. For those of you who read this book, I pray God will comfort your hearts with His Words and answer your unanswered questions."

Mae Ball, Small Business Owner

"How brave of Gracie to write down her innermost thoughts as she wrestled with God. He knew all along that her words would one day be used to comfort and encourage another mom whose world has been shattered."

Teresa in Tennessee, a hurting mom

"While reviewing your book, I just had to stop and pray. Thank you for being obedient to God's leading to share such personal and intimate thoughts, feelings, insight, and advice. Your words have a quality that I find hard to describe. The pain is so palpable—but so too is your faith and hope . . . and God's love."

Dr. Bart Dahmer, Principal/Managing Partner
Innovo Publishing LLC

SHATTERED BY SUICIDE

My Conversations with God
after the Tragic Death of My Son

Written by
Gracie Thompson

Publishing

Published by Innovo Publishing LLC
www.innovopublishing.com
1-888-546-2111

Providing Full-Service Publishing Services for
Christian Authors, Artists & Organizations: Hardbacks, Paperbacks,
eBooks, Audiobooks, Music & Videos

SHATTERED BY SUICIDE
My Conversations with God after the Tragic Death of My Son
Copyright © 2011 by Gracie Thompson
All rights reserved.

Scripture taken from...
The Message. Copyright 1993, 1994, 1995, 1996, 2000, 2001, 2002. Used by permission of
NavPress Publishing Group. **Amplified Bible**. Copyright, 1954, 1958, 1962, 1964, 1965,
1987 by The Lockman Foundation. All rights reserved. Used by permission. **New
International Version.** Scripture taken from the Holy Bible, New International Version,
Copyright 1973, 1978, 1984 by Biblica, Inc.™ Used by permission. All rights reserved
worldwide. **The Clear Word**. Copyright 2003 by Jack J. Blanco. All rights reserved. **New
King James Version**. Copyright, © 1982 by Thomas Nelson, Inc. Used by permission. All
rights reserved. **New Living Translation (NLT)** – Holy Bible, New Living Translation
copyright, 1996, 2004. Used by permission of Tyndale House Publishers, Inc. Wheaton,
Illinois 60189. **Today's New International Version** - Copyright © 2001, 2005 by Biblica.
All rights reserved worldwide. **Contemporary English Version®** - Copyright © 1995
American Bible Society. All rights reserved. **New Century Version.** Copyright © 2005 by
Thomas Nelson, Inc. Used by permission. All rights reserved. **New American Standard®**,
Copyright © 1960, 1962, 1963, 1968, 1971, 1972, 1973, 1975, 1977, 1995 by The Lockman
Foundation. Used by permission.

ISBN 13: 978-1-936076-57-4
ISBN 10: 1-936076-57-8

Cover Design & Interior Layout: Innovo Publishing LLC

Printed in the United States of America
U.S. Printing History

First Edition: February 2011

For Such a Time as This

". . . do not flatter yourself that you shall escape
. . . if you keep silent at this time,
relief and deliverance shall arise . . . from elsewhere,
but you and your father's house will perish.
And who knows but that you have come
. . . for such time as this . . .?"
Esther 4:13–14, AMP

Dear Heavenly Father,
I felt a tug on my heart as I read Esther's story.
You were working undercover in the kingdom to bring about
each circumstance, and Esther being chosen
as queen, was huge.

She agreed to put her life on the line to save her people.
To come uninvited before the king
could easily have been her death sentence . . .
but she stepped forth in faith.

I do not face an earthly king, but I face You, the King of Heaven.
You are calling me to step out of my private silence to write;
something I have never studied or practiced
or even thought about . . . until now.

I remember asking You to give me something to say—a personal
testimony that would have a greater purpose.
I got what I asked for, but it is bitter to my tongue
and almost fatal to my heart.

My testimony, my story, is about the loss of my son to suicide.
What an ugly, horrible tragedy and yet from it,
has come an awesome responsibility to share it.

The silence of suicide must be broken.
It is time to step forward and share what You have given me to write
so that other families who suffer from loss can see You,
how much You love them,
and how tenderly You hold them while they grieve.

You have so much love in Your heart
for every person on earth—all are Your precious children,
and You want them to know the Truth.

You give me the words, Father, and I will be Your scribe.
This assignment is too big for me alone
. . . I will need You every step of the way.
Thank You for trusting me—this mound of clay.

Love You Forever,
Your Daughter and Mother of Your Sons

The Journey Begins

*"Whether you turn to the right or to the left, your ears will hear a voice
behind you, saying, "'This is the way; walk in it.'"*
Isaiah 30:21, NIV

Dear Lord,
My life has taken a terrible turn.
More than ever, I need to have my ears tuned
to hear only Your voice speaking to me,
for I know not how or where to take the next step.

We begin a unique journey together
and if I did not have You walking beside me,
and often holding me up, I would not make it.
Our son's death shocked our family to the core and changed us forever.
I will never be the same . . . but I have You,
and if I walk in Your circle of Light,
I will see the path clearly.

This is not an easy journey.
Our son's sudden death caused those of us who love
him unspeakable pain.

But I feel You, Lord, guiding me
right into the eye of the storm of grief
to face it head on, to write about it, and to be healed
by Your mercy and grace.

And so we begin this journey together
with excerpts from a letter I wrote to my son.
I had so many things to say, and I could no longer speak to him
on this earth, so I wrote:

My Dear Son,

We are witnessing the beautiful colors of fall and yet each day seems to drag by without my having the slightest interest or energy to absorb the beauty. Nearly every day I shed some tears, just remembering that we no longer have you. The pictures that come to my mind are still achingly painful. I have not yet been able to move back in time to more pleasant pictures of you.

We are surrounded by friends who care, and yet I feel terribly alone. I think about joining you, but I know how much grief your death has caused us. My death would increase the family's pain and I can't do that. I must trust God to take care of each one of us who remain. I must leave the dying to Him. He is the Author of life, not death, and I know that He grieves for you too.

Perhaps, son, you suffered deeply in your heart for years and had been unable to talk to anyone about those feelings. Perhaps the one you dared to trust, a girlfriend, ended up betraying you. She probably regrets many things.

We will never know why you took your life, not on this earth anyway. But we know that Jesus loves the crushed in spirit (Psalm 34:18) and you were crushed in spirit. He cares for the brokenhearted and we are all heartbroken. We hope and pray that time will heal our hearts.

We will never forget you. I look forward to the day when we can meet again and never have to be separated. You will be in perfect health, no longer tormented by the enemy who probably tormented you for many years of your young life. It hurts not to have you in our lives, but at least you are in no more pain. You now rest until Jesus comes and He has marked your spot. He created you. He redeemed you with His blood and He is the only One who can wake you up when He returns.

I long to see you and talk with you again. This letter is a poor substitute. The only reminder we have on this earth is a small square in a cemetery nearby. We visit you often, but you don't know we are there. I have a potted, yellow mum sitting there now. It reminds me of the sunshine in your smile. I love you with all my heart, precious boy. You left us too soon.

Love you always, forget you never,
Mom

INDEX OF LETTERS

Laments

The Cry of Our Hearts

God grieves over His children:

"My people are hell-bent on leaving Me.
They pray to god Baal for help. He doesn't lift a finger to help them.
But how can I give up on you, Ephraim?
How can I turn you loose, Israel?

". . . I can't bear to even think such thoughts.
My insides churn in protest.
And so I'm not going to act on My anger.
I'm not going to destroy Ephraim. And why?
Because I am God and not a human.
I'm The Holy One and I'm here—in your very midst."
Hosea 11:7–9, MSG

King David grieves over the loss of his son:

"The king was stunned. Heartbroken, he went up to the room over the gate and
wept. As he wept he cried out,
'O my son Absalom, my dear, dear son Absalom!
Why not me rather than you, my death and not yours?
O Absalom, my dear, dear son!'"
2 Samuel 18:33, MSG

Jesus grieves over Jerusalem:

"O Jerusalem, Jerusalem, the city that kills
the prophets and stones God's messengers!
How often I have wanted to gather your children together
as a hen protects her chicks beneath her wings,
but you wouldn't let Me."
Matthew 23:37, NLT

Jesus cries to His Father:

"And at the ninth hour Jesus cried with a loud voice,
'Eloi, Eloi, lama sabachthani?'—which means
My God, My God, why have You forsaken Me
[deserted Me and left Me helpless and abandoned]?"
Mark 15:34, AMP

The cry of our hearts:

"My God, my God, why have You forsaken me?
Why are You so far from saving me,
so far from the words of my groaning?"
Psalm 22:1, NIV

Dear Heavenly Father,
I get it now.

Loss didn't begin with me on earth.
It began with You, in heaven.
Losing Lucifer and so many of Your angels must have
caused You horrible anguish.

I picked out just a few scriptures in Your precious Word that
speak of Your grief and ours, but there are many more.
These especially touched a resounding chord in my heart as they
have echoed and reechoed down through the ages in these pages;
cried out by so many of Your children.

I can relate so profoundly to the pain of King David.
I wept when I read his words,
the ones he cried when he heard of his son's death.
They were the exact words I have said over and over
since our son died.
It is devastatingly painful to reveal that I also said them
to my son before he took his life.

So he knew that I would gladly have given my life to save his . . .
only I could not do it then and I cannot do it now.
Only Jesus can save a life.

He must have agonized over His decision to save us
before His crucifixion,
according to His Words written above.

They read with such profound pain as if they were
literally ripped from His throat.
What a struggle! What a gift He gives to us!

And because He died . . . and lives, we can live;
though we first must die.
I couldn't save my son, but Your Son Jesus can . . . and did.
What a totally selfless act!
What an awesome sacrifice for Love!
Thank You, Father and Son, for Your gift of eternal life.

Why Did He Do It?

Lord, why did he do it?
I'm probably not going to get an answer
. . . at least not one that I could even begin
to accept this side of heaven.

My mind understands that my first-born son chose
to end his life.
But my heart still cries.

It cries for his pain that I could not stop.
It cries because he thought there was no other way
to end his pain.

Reasoning, I get. You and I have written about it—
but my mother heart still cries.
It cries bitter tears for all the beautiful days he's missing out on.

It cries for the college degree he will never have the chance
to spread his wings in the job market with, or
the woman he could have met who would have loved,
understood, and accepted him just the way he was.

And I shed tears for all the sweet grandchildren
we will never get to enjoy.

I look at his picture with his big grin—
and my heart breaks.
I see other brothers pummeling each other—obviously
acting like brothers—
and my heart breaks.
I pick up his billfold and finger each personal
piece of paper—
and my heart breaks.
I go to the cemetery and look down at the slab of marble with
his name engraved in bronze—
and my heart breaks.

I hear of other suicide deaths on the news—
and my heart breaks for the loved ones left behind
to pick up the pieces.

Lord, how can we blend together the business of daily toil
with heartbreak?

Life is a mixture of pain and joy, suffering and comfort,
tragedy and peace.

How do we blend them together to make an emulsion
When they are opposites, like oil and water?

That is where You come in, isn't it?
You are the "glue" that holds us together
in the midst of our times of joy and trouble.

Lord, I can guarantee that there will be more sadness and tears,
but with Your huge arms wrapped around me,
we can walk this journey together and when it ends,
it will be all joy and no more tears.
You've promised.

*"He will wipe all tears from their eyes, and there will be no more
death, suffering, crying, or pain.
These things of the past are gone forever."*
Revelation 21:4, CEV

My Son, My Son

I weep for you today, my son.
It doesn't have to be a special day
or even a special moment for me to weep—
I just have to have a fleeting thought about you.

But today, we are nearing another anniversary
of your death and so my thoughts of you are sad ones.
I miss you.
We all miss you.

Time may heal some wounds, but not these.
These wounds we suffer are endless . . .
timeless.

Losing a child is horrific; ask any parent.
Our lives go on and we may have bits of joy now and then,
but you are never far from my thoughts.
I can't help it; I'm a mom
and that is just the way I am wired.

God gave me a heart to love compassionately, completely,
and my heart did not stop loving you after yours stopped beating.
I suspect it will remain so
until mine stops.

Perhaps through my blurry eyes,
I can get a glimpse of my Heavenly Father's tears . . .
the ones He shed when His Son died on Calvary.

His Son sits at His right hand now in heaven
. . . how wonderful for us that this is so!

Even though I cry often for you
. . . and heaven cries along with me
. . . because Jesus lives, you will too!
We can't wait to see you again.
I suspect I will cry then too, but they will be tears of joy!

Rest on, son, rest on.
Your friend, Jesus, will call you soon, very soon.
Your family will be there to greet you
with arms full of hugs and faces full of kisses.

You won't know how much time has passed,
so we will have to give you an update . . . if you even care.
Then it will be home to eternity
where we will likely lose all track of time.
Hallelujah!

Surviving Suicide

They call us "survivors" and that's a good word, right?
It sure beats the other extreme
. . . and most who survive some calamity
are no doubt grateful to be one.

We are in a special class of survivors.
We are known as "suicide survivors"
but no matter how you slice it,
suicide is an ugly, repulsive word.

We are not in a category that brings relief.
We are in a class of people who survive unbearable, painful loss—
one day at a time.
One day at a time.

Perhaps you are one of us; we are millions strong.
We are parents, siblings, friends,
relatives, co-workers, and school chums.
The list is endless.
Our loved one touched so many lives, just like yours.
Why are we millions strong?
Because every fifteen minutes in the USA alone,
someone reaches the point of no return
and ends his life.

Perhaps you had just said "talk with you later" on the phone
or you sent a text message or an e-mail.
Perhaps you had made plans to play golf the next week
or go out to lunch.
Perhaps you were making plans to celebrate a birthday
together or take a trip.

And just that quickly, all plans, hopes, and dreams
vanished into thin air,
sucking the breath out of your lungs along with them.

No time to prepare.
No time to ask questions or seek advice
or suggest help for the one you love.
One day he appears fine and the next day he is gone.

No good-byes.
No understanding why.
Nothing left but emptiness, pain, heartbreak, and despair.

Why, Lord? Why?

Why Me, Lord?
But Then I Ask, Why Not Me?

Remember my prayer, Lord?
Save my children at all cost?
I never thought praying that prayer
would lead to death.
But that's what happened.

We buried one of our children—Your child.
Out of my tears and agony I sobbed,
"Why *me*, Lord. Why?
He had his whole life before him.
Why now, when it seemed
he was lingering in the valley of indecision?"

Silence. No answer came.
We slogged on, picking up the pieces
as best we could.
Life is for the living, but we were barely surviving.

As bad as our pain has been,
would we wish this gnawing grief on anyone else?
The answer had to be, "No."

So should my question be, "Why *not* me?"

To which Jesus answered softly,
"This is the work of the enemy.
I created and Love each and every one of My precious children."

"But is that all the time we get with him, Lord?" I implored.
"Sorry, but it wasn't long enough, not even close."

I pause and take a look back . . .

I was a self-sufficient Christian then, but no longer.
My heart shattered that day into confetti-like bits of flesh,
and I fell on my face begging God to extend His mercy.
Who else could understand my wailing and tears?
Are you listening, Lord?

Long, long ago before Adam and Eve were created,
the heavenly council met somewhere in the heavens.
There had to be a back-up plan
. . . just in case the humans God was going to design,
would choose to follow a different path.

Who could do the job?
Who would willingly volunteer to give His life
to pay the ultimate price for sin?

Jesus pushed His chair back from the table and stood up.

"I'll do it, Father," He said.
"If sin demands blood, then let My blood pay the ransom."

And it was done.
Council adjourned.

Fast forward about four thousand years
to the Garden of Gethsemane.
Jesus is on His face,
begging His Father for mercy.

*"Father, if possible, let there be another way,
but if not, I will keep the promise I made long ago.
They are worth every drop of blood I shed for them."*

So my question must be, "Why *not* me?"

Fast forward to the present.

The scene is full of indescribable pain
as parents, siblings, and friends say "good-bye"
to a son, brother, and friend they loved so much.

But we weren't alone in our grief and pain.
We were wrapped in the loving arms of Jesus,
while He gently wiped away the tears from our eyes
with His nail-scarred hands.

"It won't be long," He whispered softly.
*"Soon I will come and raise him up and you will have
all of eternity together.*

*Please hold on to My promises.
Please try to comprehend that he had been in terrible pain
for so long.
The enemy took pleasure in harassing him.
His grip on life . . . and on Me were getting weaker.*

*I could not bear to watch Satan make fun of him any longer.
It was time to let him take a nap.
He's safe, at peace,
and I have the best part of him—his DNA.*

*So don't worry.
He will be much better than you ever remembered.
His face will be lit with the glory of his Heavenly Father
and you will recognize his beautiful, blue eyes
and his cute little chuckle when he laughs.
I made him once . . . I can make him again.*

*Yes, My Child, you are right when you could finally ask,
'Why not me?'
I couldn't stand his pain . . . and yours hurts Me too,
but we have each other.
And you will continue to grow in My Love and understanding.*

There are many who need to hear your story.
They are everywhere—trying to bear their terrible grief in silence,
guilt, embarrassment, and shame.

They need to hear from your lips—your story.
They need to hear about the Love that never lets you go."

Love, Jesus

Grace Enough

Dear God,
You know I am the weakest of the weak
with year after year of poor health taking its toll.
And the day I heard the news that our oldest child had taken his life
was the day I thought I would surely die.

I felt like death, tasted death.
It saturated me within and clung to my pores.
Nothing can prepare someone for sudden death, absolutely nothing.
There is no script, no Cliffs Notes, no owner's manual.
You face the lion's den of death alone . . .
except for Him.

God, if Your precious Son had not faced it first . . . and rose again,
we'd have no reason to go on living.
What would be the use?

Because He lives . . . so can we.
And it is grander than anything this life will ever have to offer.
It is life eternal . . . life forever!

But until then . . . there is life to live;
it goes on in spite of tragedy.

13

So how do we accomplish this?
We do it in Your strength don't we, God?

The apostle Paul had problems many times over.
I'll let him tell us a portion of his story in his own words:
"Satan's angel did his best to get me down;
what he in fact did was push me to my knees.
No danger then of walking around high and mighty!
At first I didn't think of it as a gift, and begged God to remove it.
Three times I did that, and then He told me,

'My grace is enough; it's all you need.
My strength comes into its own in your weakness.'

"Once I heard that, I was glad to let it happen.
I quit focusing on the handicap and began appreciating the gift.
It was a case of Christ's strength moving in on my weakness.
I just let Christ take over!
And so the weaker I get, the stronger I become."
2 Corinthians 12:7–10, MSG

Like the apostle Paul, I too asked for the aching suffering of loss
to be removed, taken far away from me; but instead,
He has blessed me with strength for the journey.

But I don't walk alone . . . He walks beside me with His
muscular arm around my shoulder.
What a loving God we serve!
Thank You, God.

Surviving the Stigma

"I am scorned by all my enemies
and despised by my neighbors—even my friends
are afraid to come near me.
When they see me on the street, they run the other way."
Psalm 31:11, NLT

Dear Lord,
I know David is writing about his personal enemies . . .
and I never thought I had enemies and perhaps I don't.
But there are days when I feel just like David.
It seems that every person I meet runs the other direction.

Society may show more understanding and acceptance
than it did in previous generations,
but we still feel sort of contagious.
There lingers a stigma about suicidal death.

Not only have we lost our son to a tragic death,
but we have also lost
family, friends, and acquaintances.
Family members disagreed with our choices
and chose to step outside the family circle—
maybe due to their sorrow and confusion . . .
but what about our sorrow?

We lost our son!
Our youngest lost his only brother!

Why blame the parents?
Why blame anyone at such an awful time?

I lost my precious son.
The grave swallowed him up.

All that remains is grief, pain, suffering, sorrow,
and now we are forced to face guilt and shame?
Yes, shame for the way he died.
It's as if the enemy, through familiar voices, shouts at us:

Shame on **you** for allowing this to happen!
Why weren't **you** more watchful?
Couldn't **you** see that he was about to snap?

Why didn't **you** call in the professionals?

Don't **you** know the grave does not release those who kill themselves?
How could **you** embarrass us this way?
You are no longer welcome in our family.
Stay away!

Waves of pain roll over me as I write these words.
Remembering puts a bitter taste in my mouth
and brings tears to my eyes.
How could family members ever treat grief-stricken parents
and siblings this way?
It's unthinkable, but it happened.

It's as if Satan squeezed the life out of our child and then went on
the war path to destroy everyone who
should have been there to comfort us in our time of sorrow.

Thank You, Lord, for allowing me to vent these
wretched feelings to You.
Only You can take them away forever.

I have forgiven those who hurt us
and I choose to continue to forgive them
. . . the pain and disbelief of it all runs deep.

I am not responsible for their well-being.
However, I must respect their disapproval and keep a safe
distance out of respect for their wishes.
But I am curious.

Are we all going to live in the same neighborhood in heaven?
Will we attempt to take our hard feelings with us
so we can continue to debate
who was right and who was wrong?

What matters to our tight, little family is that our son will soon
rise to meet His Creator . . . no matter what others may say!
And when we see him in the air, we will join him!
We will be ecstatic!
Our sons are together again!

Our earthly family will be recreated in a twinkling of an eye!
We will be hugging each other and our God and King who made it all
possible, and that will be enough for us.

It is so awesome and amazing how You listen
without condemnation, Lord,
and You Love unconditionally.

Please come soon.
I love and trust You so much.
Thank You for being my Everything.

*"And the ransomed of the Lord shall return and come to Zion with singing, and
everlasting joy shall be upon their heads; they shall obtain joy and gladness, and
sorrow and sighing shall flee away."*
Isaiah 35:10, AMP

One Life Remembered

It was dark outside with very few stars peaking through
a thick blanket of clouds.
And it was late.

Most humans were tucked in behind locked doors and pulled
shades, so we had the street to ourselves.
Chirping crickets and other noisy insects blended their voices
in an orchestra of sorts to serenade us
in the humid, night air.

Our footsteps beat a rhythm as we passed by
house after house.
This night walk was unique in several ways.
It was made up of a family gathered together from near and far—
all brought together for one purpose:
to mourn the loss of our son, brother, nephew, cousin, grandson.

This walk wasn't for exercise.
We had been told that there was something special for us if we
stepped outside and walked down the street.
So that is what we were doing together.

It was a moonless night with very few street lamps to light our way,
but we had light.
Nearly every home we passed by had set a candle burning
in a window, just for us.

The candles were a gift from the children
in our church.
They wanted to quietly tell us they were sad for us and in this
small, thoughtful way, share their love.

So they had decorated electric candles and added a card to each one,
and then went from house to house on our street,
asking our neighbors to join with them to
show our family their tender regard for our loss.

The card read:
"One candle in the window
One life remembered
Showing that our love, support, and prayers
are surrounding you."

One could hear muffled sobs, mostly mine.
I was powerless to stop the flow of tears as I saw the lit candles
in nearly every neighboring window.

I felt the love and prayers from each one.

It was yet another way that God was showing us His eyes
were on us and through the hearts of young
children and neighbors,
He was reaching down to hold us.

There have been many memories created during this time of sorrow
but the candles . . . some still lit in windows, including ours . . .
are a symbol and a reminder that God cares and
remembers and so do His children.

From this love gift, given to us by the children, has blossomed a
Grief Ministry in our church.
We make and distribute bereavement baskets to church members
who face a loss in their families.
And yes, within each basket, has been placed a candle with the
same message attached.
We want to keep spreading the Love of Jesus during the hard times
of loss that we face on this earth.

It is God's ministry and we intend to continue it until He comes,
and there is no longer a reason—
because there will no longer be any death!
Praise His Name!

Thirty Years Too Short

Death causes well-meaning friends to utter worn out or even
hurtful, stabbing phrases, such as
"I know how you feel."
or . . . "Time heals all wounds."

Some may go so far in their discomfort, searching for
just the right words to say, that they blurt out awful things like,
"She's in a better place."
"It must have been God's will."
"You can have more children . . . that will help ease your grief."
"Luckily, you had him as long as you did."

Or perhaps they will try to change your focus elsewhere by asking,
"Hey, where are you going on vacation?"
"I understand you have been ill. Are you better now?"
"What projects do you have going in your free time?"
"Heard any good jokes lately? I have a few . . ."

Lord, forgive them for what they say in ignorance,
for they don't know what they are doing.
Luke 23:34, paraphrased

And strengthen me to accept the truth that we are each in a
different place in our understanding of grief, which will change as
our experience increases throughout our lives.

Help me to remember that only You can change hearts . . .
and don't let me get in the way.

Fingerprints of the Enemy

"He replied to them, 'An enemy has done this . . .'"
Matthew 13:28, AMP

Thistles found their way into a bin of wheat in this story,
which sounds like something an enemy would do.
Enemies do all kinds of hurtful things.
And Satan, our most formidable enemy, has no limits to the
evil he can think up.

If we could have dusted our son's home for Satan's fingerprints,
I am certain we'd have found them, for suicide is
definitely the work of the enemy.

Satan killed someone we hold dear—our son and brother.
He has no feelings and absolutely no regard
for the sanctity of human life.
As far as he is concerned, a good human is a dead human.
Once he has used him up, he is disposable.

According to research, many suicide victims have been depressed,
either diagnosed or suspected.
Satan keeps an evil eye out for weak, easily depressed children
and preys on them throughout their lives.

After years and years of such abuse, the fragile, terrorized victims
just want the world to go away.
They are not punishing anyone and they can't begin to
comprehend the pain their death will cause others.
All they can think about is their own pain, which has become
a tightening noose of hopelessness.

No longer can they see a bright, productive future.
They have lost all hope, all reason to live . . .
and Satan is right there to nudge them over the edge
to the jagged cliffs below.
Any death is so difficult to understand, Lord.
And it is super difficult to comprehend when someone you love
takes matters into his own hands . . . completing suicide.
Help us to understand so that we can reach out
to love and support Your other children
who are suffering survivors
just like we are.

Death, though part of the enemy's scheme . . . is a nap.
You call it "the *sleep* of death" (Job 14:12, CEV).
Though we miss our son so much, he is no longer in pain.

So You turned the torment of the enemy into a much-needed rest.

Lord, You have promised to never leave or forsake us,
so please hold on to us until You come,
no matter how long it takes . . .
but please let it be soon.

We can't wait to hug You as tightly as You have hugged each of
us . . . and to be reunited with those we love so much.

Suicide

Dear Lord,
This "S" word is so ugly, I can hardly speak it.
The dictionary defines it as meaning to kill oneself *intentionally*.
I recoil from the very thought.

Who would place such a low value on themselves
or be hurting so badly that they see no other choice?
Unfortunately, the answer is many. Way too many.

Suicide is the fifth leading cause of death
among our very young, ages 5–14.
I've said it before, but it bears repeating: every fifteen minutes
another American dies by suicide.
Our son was an attempt, but he completed his.
Now he is a statistic—a painful, tragic loss that we face every day.

How it must hurt You, Lord.
Your Love is so powerful, so deep, that to have to watch one of
Your children, of any age, make such a choice
must rip Your heart out.
I think I understand a bit of what You must feel,
for I know what a broken heart feels like.

But I don't know what it feels like to witness all of Your
children hurt themselves.
One is enough to lose.
How do You stand it, Lord?
How can I stand it?

For days afterwards, I didn't think I would be able to breathe.
I certainly didn't care if I lived or died.
My child was in a cemetery where no one belongs,
and all that remains is a slab with his name on it.

Every time we replace his flowers,
we look around at the growing number of soft, fresh mounds—
a solemn reminder that death is still happening.
Those parents and families are crying fresh tears,
and I feel their pain.

All we can do now is replace our son's flowers, clip the
straggling blades of grass around his marker, and
shed quiet tears of longing and loss.

We walk around the cemetery and notice names and dates.
We set flowers upright that have dipped their heads to the
ground in sorrow. That's it. That's all we can do.
We have no more part to play in our son's life.

Now, we wait for the trumpet blast . . . You will blow
it loudly, right Lord?
Shake those graves; wake up our son!
Wake up Your children, asleep in their dusty beds!

Good morning, son! How we've longed to see you!
Jesus has come to gather you to Himself . . .
and to all the rest of us who have missed you so much.

There will be no more death, not even close.
And no more sleep . . . we'll never get tired.

Eternity has begun and it is more than we ever dreamed of.
I won't be able to stop smiling . . .
Maybe for a hundred years or even a thousand!

*"For the Lord Himself will come down from heaven, with a loud command,
with the voice of the archangel and with the trumpet call of God,
and the dead in Christ will rise first."*
I Thessalonians 4:16, TNIV

Crushed Petals

*"The LORD is close to the brokenhearted and saves those
who are crushed in spirit."*
Psalm 34:18, NIV

He was just beginning to show the maturity
of manhood, Lord.
At a young, tender age when he was yet a tight bud of promise,
his fragrance perfumed the air
. . . and now he had attained special educational goals
. . . but would never see his diploma.
We are left to wonder what happened.
His freshly opened rose was crushed before it had barely
had a chance to display its beauty.
Why God, why? Why did You let it happen?
Was his heart as crushed on the inside as his rose was
crushed on the outside?

I don't know what more you could ask of a mother who held
those fragile, bruised petals in her hands and
sobbed into their sweetness.

But I take the text above to heart,
trusting that You knew he had a broken spirit.
And You were close by, just itching to hold him if he'd let You.

He was crushed and nearly snuffed out before his death, wasn't he?
We struggle so against not knowing the details even though
more understanding would not return him to us.

He's resting now.
Resting until You call him by name.
No matter where we are when You call, please rush our family
to his side for a joyous five-way hug.

The Last Good-Bye

I don't know how to put this into words, Lord.
It has been several years, and yet the emotions still slam into
my heart and gut; wrenching me anew like it was but a few days ago.

The news was unbelievable, shocking, terrifying.
My mind dug in its heels and rebelled . . . absolutely refusing
to accept the horrifying truth.

"It has to be a mistake, please tell me it's a mistake!"

The heart is nowhere ready to receive, and yet
much is expected . . . people are waiting . . . they want answers.
We need more time . . .
We want to shift this exploding locomotive into reverse.

The burial process is brutal.
First the morgue, then the autopsy, then the funeral home . . .
and we still couldn't see him.
We still couldn't verify that he was really ours.

Then we could . . . and it was him . . . much to my fragmented
hopes and prayers to the contrary.

Lord, where are You?
How could You allow this to happen?

All the pieces are but a blur.
I remember having to greet friends and neighbors
for hours while they paid their respects.

None of it was a picnic, Lord.
All formalities when I just wanted to open up that box
and take my son home with me.

How we got through the funeral service, only You know.
How my children could stand up front and talk about their
brother, I'll never know.
They showed such strength, such pride in their brother,
and I am awesomely proud of them.

Then it was time for the last good-bye.
I both dreaded it and longed for it to be over.
I did not know how to prepare for this final ceremony any more
than I had known how to prepare for the others.

People had just taken us by the hand and led us
where we did not want to go.

And now we faced placing our beloved child and brother
in the ground . . . in the same cemetery we had driven by
hundreds of times, but never felt any emotion or connection to
. . . until now.
And it would never be the same ever again.

Now it was to be the final resting place for one of our children.
Never could we pass by again
without feeling our hearts
jump to our throats.
Either we stop and cry and check his flowers,

or we pass by slowly, craning our necks to look for the bright
flower arrangements that mark his special spot against the
backdrop of leafy green.

But right now,
we are getting out of our cars and walking slowing to the canopy.
Shouldn't this gathering be for someone else?
Someone we don't know, but casually feel sorry for
as we drive by?

The director gets out of his vehicle and catches up to us.
He has a strange, velvet-covered box in his hands.
"Would anyone like to carry this?" he asks.

Our youngest has grown up years in the last week.
He has done things to relieve our minds—
things that had to hurt him deeply.
But he is the first to respond,
"Yes, I'll carry it."

I watch as he clutches it tightly to his chest
with both arms wrapped snuggly around it as if it is fragile and
might break should it slip from his grasp and fall to the ground.

His face is filled with tender emotion . . . as tears run
unchecked down his cheeks.
How I ache to hold him, to comfort him, to tell him it will all be
okay, but I cannot change this day, or I would.
Oh God, You know I would.

We were ushered to our seats. My eyes were blurred with tears.
Who all was there? I couldn't see.
Mostly friends, I think . . . most family members could not stay
for this day or chose not to come.

The minister said some kind words I am sure,
but I don't remember.
I couldn't take my eyes off my son who still cradled the box . . .
and yet I did not want to stare and invade his last,
private moments with his beloved brother—his
first childhood playmate and then his grown-up bro.

The service was over and it was time to say good-bye.
Do we have to? Can't we just remain here forever?
One by one, we took a turn clutching the remains of our
precious son and brother.

We turned to leave, but not without one more symbol of
love and respect and honor . . .
A crisp salute from our oldest son who proudly
and faithfully serves our country.

It was over.
Nothing left but a smooth, granite slab with
his name and dates—
dates and a dash . . . that is all that remains . . .
until Jesus comes.
Therein lies our bright spot!
Though we mourn daily, we also have hope!
Praise God!
We have hope in eternal life and our son will jump out of his
dusty grave as soon as he hears the trumpet blast!

At last, no more sad good-byes . . . only hugs and hellos!
Oh come, Lord Jesus, and please make it soon!

Anniversaries Hurt

Anniversaries are supposed to be a celebration, Lord,
but these aren't happy anniversaries.
We miss our boy.

As the anniversary date of his death draws near,
I thought of a "weeping" text.
Jeremiah 31:15, NLT, speaks of mothers mourning for their
children because they were no more.
I can relate.

Shedding tears of grief has been a common practice for
thousands of years because we share a planet with an
enemy whose entire focus is death.

I am learning not to stop there, but to read on: ". . . But God
says, 'Stop your incessant weeping, hold back your tears . . .
There's hope for your children.'"
Jeremiah 31:16–17, MSG

When this text came to my mind today, Lord, it was as if You
placed Your strong hand gently on my shoulder and breathed
comfort and peace into my sorrowful soul.

Yes, we still have tears, but we also have reasons for joy.
Your Word says that Your eyes are on those
who hope in Your unfailing Love.

So we hopefully wait for You, Lord, our Help and our Shield.
Psalm 33:18 & 20, NIV, paraphrased

Hair-Pin Curve

We heard the whine of his engine;
it had to be one of those "crotch rockets" approaching
at a high rate of speed.
It was so dark out . . . why wasn't he slowing down
for the curve? Then crash!

It was late. We could see the field covered with bright lights
from fire engines and rescue vehicles.
But sadly, there was to be no rescue this night.

They were trying to map out what happened—trying to make
sense out of a senseless decision
that snuffed out the life of a young man in an instant.
The family had to be in shock and agony . . . and oh how we
understood and grieved with them.

The morning after, I took a walk down to the scene.
It was peaceful and quiet except for the birds singing a happy
song. There were no reminders of an impact except for
chalk markings on the grass.

The only remaining reminder to those who pass by that spot
is a small, white cross with his name written on it . . . along with
notes and signatures and flowers from
those who love him.

It's so senseless, Lord.
My heart cries for this family as Yours does.
They lost a son. Dad lost a business partner.
Sister lost a twin brother . . .
And he had a tiny child.

Lord, we aren't the only ones who grieve.
But we have You. Do they?

Every time I pass that little white cross, still
surrounded by flowers,
I remember the family is in pain and I send up a prayer.

Only You can comfort them, Lord, so please wrap Your
huge arms around them and hold them until
they are quieted and at peace.

Healing a Broken Heart

Dear Heavenly Father,
This title is so personal that it hurts.
This is my heart we are talking about.
It is mending . . . slowly . . .
but most days, it still feels broken anew.

I speak for myself and my family.
I speak for those who have not yet found their voice;
their pain is too fresh, too great.
And I speak for all who felt they had no way out except to
end their tortured lives.

How sad for all of us, Father.
Please hold us when we cry.
Please collect all our tears in Your bottle (Psalm 56:8, NLT).
Please pick us up before we falter and fall.
Some days, I hear Your sweet voice speaking softly in my ear,

My Blessed Child, I do weep when you weep.
Your grief has reached heaven and Our sadness matches yours.
But all is not lost.
We know what awaits you and your child
who was laid to rest.
He is taking a dirt nap, and for him,
it will seem like it just began . . .

He won't remember the time.
And he won't think to ask any more than you will.
You see, My coming will be so stunning,
so spectacular that nothing you have ever experienced
will compare.

Weep on, My Child, until relief comes . . . I have plenty of bottles.
Just know that weeping will not last forever.
It will end and then the joy will follow—
a new morning filled with fantastic joy!

We Couldn't Bear to Lose Him

Dear Lord,
I feel you urging me to write about feelings I'd rather keep hidden—
memories from a painful time
that remain embedded in my heart like barbed arrows.

I have pushed this conversation deep down into the darkest part
of my soul . . . hoping to never have to deal with it again,
but You are persistent . . . and You know my heart
better than I do.

If I could roll back time and begin about a week before our son's
tragic and untimely death,
I'd come to a few days of vacation he had off from work.
He decided to come home and spend them with us.

Of course, we were elated.
He usually spent a quick weekend once in a while,
so it would be wonderful to have some extra time with him.
He planned a golf game and other things family and friends
enjoyed doing together, but something was off . . .
way off.

He had sent us a copy of an e-mail
that he had also sent to his girlfriend.
It was both frightening and heartbreakingly sad.
She had broken up with him and he was not taking her decision
well at all and threatened to hurt himself . . .

I was eager to see him and check him out for myself.
He was not his usual chipper self and withdrew often to be alone,
even when family or friends were around.

How he was really doing was always, always on my mind.
How could I help him?
He was already seeing a therapist so that was encouraging,
I thought.

Did the recent golf game cheer him up?
He seemed to have a good time, at least that was what
I was told by my husband.

But later my son and I had a private talk and he
poured out words of heartache between sobs that wracked his body.
I rubbed his back, hugged him, and tried to console him.

Our conversation naturally weighed heavily on my mind and heart
after he had returned home.
There was nagging fear . . . deep in my gut.

I sat down to share the details with my husband.
He listened to my worry about our son's pain and my quandary
as to whether or not we should push into his life
to try to help him.
After all, he was a grown man with rights to his
own life and privacy.

I expected to hear my husband echo my fears, so what he
did say, shocked me.

"Did he say anything about the golf game?" he asked.
Golf? Golf? That's all you care about here!! Were you listening?
Aren't you concerned about your son's welfare?

But I did not ask those questions out loud.
He didn't seem to be alarmed by anything I had said
and I did not have the energy to tell it to him all over again;
not now anyway.

We had planned to go see our son and celebrate his birthday
the following weekend.
Perhaps we could talk further with him then.
Unbeknown to us, he would be dead before the weekend.

I've had to stop and cry my heart out as I write this.
The deep ache of remorse is still there, wounding me,
and the "why" questions linger.
Perhaps I could have done something to stop it . . .

Why was I "pushed" to write about this, God?
Was I to write it down so I could hurt all over again?
There are no answers to our endless questions so what's the point
of recording it in black and white?
How can there be any benefit to come from this agony?

Dear Daughter,
My arms are wrapped around you as you type
and I will hold you while you sob.
My tears mingle with yours . . . I miss him, too!

Remember My friend Lazarus?
I was moved to tears then too, even though I knew I was going
to wake him up within minutes.

Since My time frame is different from yours,
I will tell you that it will seem only like a few minutes since your
son's death before I will be waking him up again!

My Dear Daughter, your grief is temporary,
this world is temporary,
death and the enemy are temporary,
so hold on to Me!

Forgive your husband for his thinking . . .
He has played this conversation over and over in his mind, too . . .
trying to make sense of it all.

You both love your son so much and I know that . . .
And your love is just the beginning of My great Love for him.
I took him to save him . . . there was no other way.

He had suffered many years, from childhood on . . .
from taunts and threats by the enemy; things he neither understood
nor knew how to put into words.

It would not have been long and the enemy
would have pushed him over the edge
and far away from eternity,
so I stepped in.

I knew how much his death would hurt all of you who love him,
but try to understand that I had to let him
take a rest to save him for eternity.

Dad and I talked often about his struggle; We knew the enemy
was closing in for the kill . . . it was time.

This is how Dad put it: "Son, we have delayed as long as we dare.
We must move quickly before the enemy strikes.
We can't bear to lose him for all eternity, so let's snatch him away from
Satan now and save him forever. He's Our boy!"

I know you are in agony, precious daughter. I am too.
But remember that Satan does not have the last word here . . .
I do.

I AM the Author and the Finisher of your faith (Hebrews 12:2, NKJV)
and the Victor over sin and death (1 Corinthians 15:57, NLT).

So weep when you need to and I will always
be there to comfort you.
Put your hope in eternity where I Am . . . and where your son will be . . .
all brand new and ready to live forever.

Love,
Jesus

"But your dead will live; their bodies will rise.
You who dwell in the dust, wake up and shout for joy.
Your dew is like the dew of the morning;
the earth will give birth to her dead."
Isaiah 26:19, NIV

It's That Time Again

We are rounding another calendar year and heading
for that horrible milestone.
Dear Lord, why is it still so hard?

For days now, I find myself dreading the approaching
date worse than I dread a root canal.
I am a basket of tears, becoming emotional even with totally
unrelated topics.
No one would dare mention our loss now . . .
and they rarely do any other time of the year.

Do I sound bitter?
Perhaps I am . . . just a little, or a lot, I'm not sure.
But the awful memories come up and choke me this
month more than any other in the year.

Perhaps I let them, more than any other time too.
The loss of our son was so horrible and we miss him so much,
even though we have come to accept his death
better now than we did.

I try to have good memories about him . . .
and his dad and I talk about those a lot. It helps.
But the family members who fell away from us . . . over his death,
never speak of him to us.
I can't seem to find good memories to erase those ugly ones.

My mind understands
that each of Your children is Your responsibility,
but my heart still hurts for all the things said and done during
those few, awful days we were all together.

Lord, do those memories ever cross their minds?
Do they look at the calendar, realizing that the anniversary date
of our son's death is approaching and feel any remorse?
I don't doubt that they loved him and miss him,
but do they feel any sorrow for the way they treated us?
Is it guilt, Lord, that keeps them silent?

There are no answers to these questions.
Perhaps I am not supposed to wonder, but I can't help it.
I do wonder.

I dread the day, but dreading won't keep it from coming.
I will try to occupy myself with other things
and with You by my side,
I will get through it.
That's my goal. Simple, and yet loaded.

You are the only One I can count on that day, right?

You have been with me all the days . . . before and after . . .
even though I must admit that there are many times
when I have felt all alone.
Please remind me that I am not.

Please remind me that You will carry me through this anniversary
like You carried me through the others.
And please remind me that You won't forget to return.
Please remind me that it will be soon.

I have nothing else I can count on but Your return.
And then, any lingering memories will vaporize when
I first see Your face and then see my son's face . . . together.
Now won't that be a scene to commit to memory
and savor for all eternity?

To the Brink . . . and Back

*"Jesus was taken into the wild by the Spirit for the test.
The devil was ready to give it . . .*

*For the second test the devil took Him to the Holy City.
He sat Him on top of the Temple and said,
'Since You are God's Son, jump.'*

*The devil goaded Him by quoting Psalm 91:
'He has placed You in the care of angels.
They will catch You so that You won't so much as
stub Your toe on a stone.'
Jesus countered with another citation from Deuteronomy:*

'Don't you dare test the Lord your God.'"
Matthew 4:1, 5–7, MSG

It was hard those first few months after our son's death
to even think of a reason to leave the house.
I didn't want to go anywhere, but I didn't want to stay.
I was falling, falling into nothingness
. . . with no way to get my bearings
. . . and I did not care.

But after some time passed
we finally took the opportunity to get away.
The exercise and fresh air did us both good.

As my eyes gazed upward into the deep blue sky and rugged
ridges of the hills around us,
I felt God's Presence in a way I had not felt it in a long time.
I could begin to relax and trust Him;
ready and willing to listen in case
He spoke to my barren soul.

One early morning, I was walking alone.
I had ventured higher than I had before,
leaning in and digging my toes in the loose gravel to keep my
footing on the steep climb.
I paused to catch my breath,
sucking in deep draughts of crisp, clean air.

The woods were thick and hard for my eyes to penetrate,
but in them were sure to be eyes looking back at me . . . wild ones.
This was God's country where wild animals roamed freely
in their habitat.
I was very much aware that I was stepping into their domain,
so being alone, I thought I should turn back
and head down the trail.

Going down was easier, but still I had to proceed cautiously in
the soft dirt mixed with gravel under my feet.

Round the bend, I could look down off a ridge and my tummy
did a flip flop as I realized how far up I had climbed.
And just at that moment, a voice spoke clearly in my head,
"Go ahead, jump. You can end your misery right now and join
him. No one will know . . . and they won't
find your body for days.
Do it!"
Stunned, I sucked in my breath and couldn't let it out for a few
seconds as my mind whirled, trying to comprehend
what I had just heard.

Certainly God wouldn't say such a thing
. . . so it had to be . . . Satan!
Yes, it must have been Satan goading me to end my life
. . . stop the pain!

When I felt strength return to my legs,
I hurried back down to my husband and safety.
That was a strong directive, and I realized then and there
that the enemy would never leave us alone.

He had taken one of our precious children,
but he wouldn't stop there.
He would take anyone else too and will continue to try
. . . not only in our family, but in yours, too!

"Jesus' refusal was curt: *'Beat it, Satan!'"*

He backed His rebuke with a third quotation from Deuteronomy:

*"'Worship the Lord Your God, and only Him.
Serve Him with absolute single-heartedness.'*

The Test was over.
The devil left. And in his place, angels!
Angels came and took care of Jesus' needs."
Matthew 4:10–11, MSG

Every Breath I Take

Ever thought about every breath you take?
Me neither.
Breathing in and out is a natural response we take for granted.
We certainly don't remember taking our first birth breath
outside our mother's womb.

Like Job, I am slowly learning how to not even take the gift of
breath for granted.
Job spoke from his own experience when he said,
"We bring nothing at birth; we take nothing with us at death.
The Lord alone gives and takes . . ." (Job 1:21, CEV).

Even if the hearse pulls a U-Haul
full of my earthly possessions behind it,
I will have no cognizance of it, for where I am going . . .
I will know nothing (Ecclesiastes. 9:5, NIV paraphrased).

I am not trying to sound morbid, but breath is a gift.
And until Jesus returns, death is the enemy who stares us all
down until he seizes an opportunity to snuff out our breath.

We had to face the unimaginable when our son died.
Suddenly, the scriptures about death and life became very important.

The Bible says that the dead know not anything—period.
So my son may have been troubled in life,
but in death he is at peace.

Jesus compares death to sleep (John 11:11, NIV).
And we comfort one another with these words
(1 Thessalonians 4:18, AMP).

I look at breathing differently now.
Each breath of air is precious and necessary to maintain life,
and my life should have a point.

It should be more than a dash between two dates.

God created me for His purpose
and I desire, now more than ever before,
to know His plan for my life.

Doing what He has designed for me to do will bring
us closer to His coming and it gives Him
. . . and therefore, me . . .the greatest pleasure.
Philippians 2:12, MSG, paraphrased

Even though I continue to grieve, God is there to console me
and to help me press on, spreading His Good News.

Along with Job, I can say,
"Praise the name of the Lord!"
Job 1:21, CEV

No Trespassing

Dear Jesus,
I thought I'd tell you that I have buried my painful memories in a
deep hole in an obscure part of my property,
and I posted a "No Trespassing" sign.

I hope You don't plan on snooping around there or anything.
I've been stuffing pain all my life and that is the way I deal with
my problems; I have to move on.
That bag was filled to overflowing after tragedy struck so I piled
it in the back of my pick-up and buried it in my field.

No one knows where it is except me . . . and obviously You do too.
But leave it alone, please.
It's better that way.
What good does it do to go digging around in the past?
What's happened has happened . . . it is what it is.

My Dear Child,
Your heart will always be where your treasure is.
Remember the story in Matthew?
This story is referring to storing our valuables in heaven
rather than on earth,
but memories are treasure too, even sad ones.
The heart remembers and wants to go there to unlock the pain
and deal with it, and be set free.
You asked that I not snoop around and I won't,
not without your permission.
But remember that unearthing trash or treasure
is one of My specialties.
Together, we can sort what is to be saved and what is to be tossed.
Giving Me freedom to help you will bring you to
freedom and lasting peace.
Think about it.

Love,
Jesus

"For where your treasure is, there will your heart be also."
Matthew 6:21

Just a Touch

"A woman who had suffered a condition of hemorrhaging for twelve years—a long succession of physicians had treated her, and treated her badly, taking all her money and leaving her worse off than before— had heard about Jesus.

She slipped in from behind and touched His robe.
She was thinking to herself,
'If I can put a finger on His robe, I can get well.'

The moment she did it, the flow of blood dried up.
She could feel the change
and knew her plague was over and done with.

At the same moment, Jesus felt energy discharging from Him.
He turned around to the crowd and asked,

'Who touched My robe?'
His disciples said, 'What are You talking about?
With this crowd pushing and jostling You, You're asking, "Who touched Me?"
Dozens have touched You!'

But He went on asking, looking around to see who had done it.
The woman, knowing what had happened, knowing she was the one,
stepped up in fear and trembling, knelt before Him,
and gave Him the whole story.

Jesus said to her,
'Daughter, you took a risk of faith, and now you're healed and whole.
Live well, live blessed! Be healed of your plague.' "
Mark 5:25–34, MSG

Dear Lord,
Like the afflicted woman in the bustling crowd who touched the
hem of Your garment and was instantly healed,
I am reaching, straining with the tips of my fingers to touch You
for I too desire complete healing, inside and out.

Her faith was instantly rewarded . . . how awesome!
To be able to glorify You with such a testimony from my lips
would be wonderfully awesome as well.

You promise healing—
some happen instantly, others slowly over time,
and still others, like the apostle Paul to whom You said,

"My grace is enough; it's all you need.
My strength comes into its own in your weakness."
2 Corinthians 12:9, MSG

Paul responded,
"Once I heard that, I was glad to let it happen.
I quit focusing on the handicap and began appreciating the gift.
It was a case of Christ's strength moving in on my weakness.
Now I take limitations in stride, and with good cheer
. . . I just let Christ take over!"
2 Corinthians 12:10, MSG

I choose to live in Your strength too, Lord,
no matter when healing comes—either now or when You return.
But whenever it is, Lord, I now surrender completely to Your will.
Amen.

"Heal me, O Lord, and I will be healed; save me and I will be saved,
for You are the one I praise."
Jeremiah 17:14, NIV

Untouchable

My Dear Friend, Jesus,
I am ever so grateful for Your touch.
Many of us often feel untouchable by mankind.
Some of us have oozing sores, others of us have slept by the
dumpster too long and we are filthy.
Some of us walk the streets at night, trying to make a living
while others of us mourn . . . but no matter the reason,
we can feel untouchable.
And even if we are loved, it is often from a safe distance.

Some of us feel like we reside inside a chalk-drawn circle and few
venture in close enough for a touch and stay to exchange words.

Does our pain or filthy rags stop them?
Will they catch what we have?

45

Will they become contaminated if they touch our unwashed skin?
Will sorrow soon catch them if they grieve too long with us?

What makes us shy away, Lord?
Has the "tidied up and put away" focus of society caused us to
turn away from the broken down, the hobbling, the slowly dying
or keep us from venturing into the poor sections of town?

If I desire to be like You, Jesus, I will not turn away.
You didn't.

*"When He came down from the mountainside, large crowds followed Him. A
man with leprosy came and knelt before Him and said, 'Lord, if You are willing,
You can make me clean.'*

Jesus reached out His hand and touched the man,

'I am willing,' He said. 'Be clean!'

Immediately he was cured of his leprosy."
Matthew 8:1–3, NIV

You amaze me, Jesus!
You never shy away from sick, wretched conditions of any kind.
In fact, You used some pretty strong language with the teachers
of the law during the years You were on earth.

*"These people make a big show of saying the right thing, but their hearts
aren't in it. They act like they're worshiping Me but don't mean it."*
Isaiah 29:13, MSG

When I said I'd follow You no matter where You lead,
then I must follow You to the dumpster, to the poor parts of
town, into nursing homes, and into the arms of those who are
in pain, depressed, hurting, lost.
Thank You, Jesus, for Your example.
Please give me the desire to follow and the strength to be

Your hands, Your feet, Your heart to anyone
You place in my path.

Love You forever,
Your Daughter

Life Without Your "Bro"

My Dear Son,
May I ask what it's like for you?
I have written pages of what it's like for me,
but what about you?
You and your brother were two peas in a pod.
Where one of you was, there would be the other one.
And the oft used phrase, "what one of you didn't think of,
the other one did" had to have been written
about the two of you.
When you no longer played together or built things together,
you kept in touch by phone calls and e-mails.
Not that you'd tell me, but I somehow knew,
and it made me smile.
You also referred to each other not by name but
as "my brother" and I treasure those words of possession
. . . now, more than ever.
There has to be a hole in your heart after he was yanked away
so unexpectedly and horribly, by death.
I want to ask, "How are you doing?" but your
"cover" seems to be fastened down tightly.
Perhaps you wish to "move on"
or protect us from further pain, but pain is still there,
and so is my great love for you, my grown son.

Perhaps you don't yet realize that God's arm is wrapped tightly
around your shoulders too.
He will walk beside all of us through the remainder of our lives
until He takes us home to be with Him and
your beloved bro forever.
Love you forever,
Mom

Tickets

Lord, the tickets came today—football season tickets.
My husband held them proudly.
Yes, they are for the hometown team, but there's more—
and it goes much deeper.

He pointed to the address.
It was addressed to our son, the one who is
no longer with us.
I ache every time I see a piece of mail dropped in our mailbox
addressed to him.
It reminds me that he used to have a life in this life;
but he has one no longer.

My husband, on the other hand, treasures seeing the
name of our first-born son on these tickets.
They remind him of all the games
they used to attend together.

Entertainment still goes on and we must go on . . .
dragging the broken pieces of our hearts behind us.
Tickets . . .

Now, father and remaining son still go. They must go—
for the love of the game.
They smile, they laugh; they munch and sip . . .
For those few happy hours, they excitedly watch their
team score touchdown after touchdown . . . in a perfect world.

Do they remember that it used to be three of them?
Certainly, for they shared a bond—a bond of love
that cannot be broken.

So it's really not about the tickets . . .
It's about the love between a father and his sons.
The bigger picture is always about the Love of the Father
for His children; His sons and daughters.
Thank You, Father, for leading by example,
and showing us how to love.

Shredded Family Ties

Lord, my cup is full to overflowing—
full of anger, or maybe more like rage, I think.
Rage at things, events, circumstances
that I cannot control.
I'll pick one.

My son died of his own choosing—
no note, no warning, no good-byes.
The pain has been torture . . . You know of my flowing
tears, the anguish, the wishes to join him.

And if that weren't enough,
family turned their backs on us for decisions we chose to make—
had to make amidst the grief of us all.

Why, Lord?
Who said we had to choose sides?
This wasn't supposed to be a contest to see who wins.

All we, parents and children, could do for him now was to
bury him with as much dignity as possible . . .
and some family members still turned away in anger.
How dare we inconvenience them?
How dare we make decisions without
seeking their counsel?
After all, they were family, and family has rights.
Apparently as parents and children,
we didn't have the right to make our own decisions.
And these were dreadfully ugly, harsh,
and difficult decisions to make!

I have forgiven them over and over, and still there is more
forgiving that needs to be extended in this one-sided forgiveness.
My cup is still full-to-overflowing with pain, Lord.
Family members are unable to speak to us about our son
to help us all heal, and perhaps to help mend
the broken fences in our family ties.

I might describe it like a three-layer, chocolate cake—luscious
and mouth-watering.
But inside, it is filled with poisonous pain
. . . carefully covered up with a
swirled perfection of creamy fudge frosting—"anger" frosting.
The anger is a beautiful covering for all the pain
that is hidden deep inside.
That is what anger is—a covering for pain.
Anger is really a secondary emotion;
it's how we naturally react to pain.
Pain makes us vulnerable, and we want to avoid being vulnerable.

Anger makes us feel in control, strong, and capable.

In anger and pain, we look around to blame someone—
to rid ourselves of the suffocating guilt and pain.

Lord, forgive me today for all the bitterness and anger that
still rages in my broken heart.
Perhaps they have been blinded to the Truth?
Whatever it be, if they never speak to me again on this earth,
I pray that You will bring us together for a
fresh start in heaven.

Today

Today is Survivor's Day for our family.
Today we remember our son and brother and how much
we love him.
Today we reflect on special moments, trying to engrain
these stories into our minds so we can continue
to share them with those who follow after,
those who will never have the privilege of knowing him.
Today is special; it knits us closer together as a family.
Surviving suicide is not for sissies.
It takes courage to face the future with love and gratitude.
And we will, as we remain forever
in God's grip.

Please Catch Me, Lord

*"Though they stumble, they will never fall, for the Lord
holds them by the hand."*
Psalm 37:24, NLT

Lord, I have been free falling—spiraling downward for days,
months, and now years since the sudden, tragic death of our son.

Thanks to Your tender care, I am dropping down more gently
now and hopefully, I will soon land.
Please be my soft place to fall . . . right into a
cushiony cloud from heaven.

Grieving is hard work, the hardest job one could ever have.
It's not something easily understood . . . unless
you too, my friend, are grieving deeply.

I know in my head—and slowly my heart is catching up—
that You, Lord, are the Truth and our only hope.
I have often wondered over the last few years how people grieve
who do not realize that they have You to lean on.

I do know I can lean on You, and I am so grateful,
and yet the road is long and rough, full of potholes and detours.
Knowing that You are by my side and will pick me up
and carry me whenever I get tired,
is such a relief.

Lord, I desire to be strong enough to be a testimony to others
of Your healing power.
There are so many who hurt just like my family and I do.

And yet . . . they may not know that
You are the very air we breathe.
You are the wind beneath our tattered wings.
You alone heal our pain. You alone have the perfect touch.
You alone can cushion our fall.
You alone provide lasting comfort.

"Praise God, the Father of our Lord Jesus Christ!
The Father is a merciful God, who always gives us comfort."
2 Corinthians 1:3, CEV

Thank You.

Little Lost Lamb

"The Lord is my Shepherd . . ."
Psalm 23:1, NIV

My Dear Children,
You probably thought you were alone at his graveside today,
but you weren't.
I am always there beside you.
I know that you don't realize I'm there, but I want to be wherever you are to
provide comfort
to your sad and lonely hearts.

I sat beside you while you trimmed the grass the mower missed
and swept his marker clean.
I saw you adjust the flowers, or sometimes
you bring in a new bouquet.
I heard your words of longing and I saw your falling tears.

I know you can't wait to see him again, and you tell Me over and over to
"hurry up". I understand how you feel, and I know
you mean no disrespect.
I'm eager to wake him up . . . for I miss him, too.

There are thousands upon thousands of graves just like his, and their families
miss them . . . and I miss them.
I think I have told you this before, but perhaps it bears repeating.

Your son is My little lamb. He's one of My precious lambs
for whom I gave up My life, and I would do it again.

Perhaps you remember the story about the shepherd
who had 100 sheep.
He cared for them from daybreak until sunset.
He took care of their sores and pulled out briars and thorns while
always keeping a watchful eye out for predators.

One evening, as it was edging toward twilight, he called to them.
It was time for them to follow him back to the sheep pen so he could close
them in safely for the night.
He counted each one as it passed by.

"Ninety-nine, okay, where's Blackie. Come, Blackie.
Come here, boy," he called, but there was no answering bleat.

The sheep knew his voice and they always came.
They sensed that he loved them and would always be faithful
to care for their needs.

So what happened to Blackie?
Perhaps he wandered away for some choice grass
and didn't hear the shepherd call?

"I will have to go back out into the night,"
the shepherd said to himself,
"I must find my lost lamb. Yes, yes, I know
I have ninety-nine sheep and perhaps losing one would be okay
for other shepherds, but not me.
I must have all my sheep safely back in the pen."

Back out into the night he went. He called and shined his lantern into the
shadows; searching every nook and craggy ledge where
Blackie could have gotten stuck.

Suddenly, he heard a faint little "bah-bah."
It sounded like it was coming from somewhere down below.
He quickly retraced his steps on the uneven pasture, now searching for a deep
ditch or ravine
where Blackie could have fallen.

And there was the little guy, down in a hole with no way to free
his back legs and climb out.
Murmuring softly, the shepherd reached in and tugged Blackie free and put
the fuzzy, little fellow around his neck.

*Blackie's heart was beating wildly, and he kept licking the back of his
master's neck and everywhere else he could reach;
he was so happy to be free.
And his master was equally delighted
to have found his little lost lamb.*

*See, Children, I will never give up on My sheep;
they are My children.
I would have died for just one of My lost children.
You are worth far more than little Blackie and the shepherd who
refused to leave him alone out in the cold.*

*You see, your son . . . and he is My son too . . . he is My lamb.
He's one I died to save and I want him
in My heavenly sheep pen.
Eternity wouldn't be complete without him, and I know you want
your entire family together in heaven and so do I.*

*I have many sheep to gather in, and I know you want to help
Me do that great task.
Keep writing, keep learning, keep trusting, and keep growing in
our friendship, which is so precious to Me.*

*My Spirit dwells within you.
I Love you passionately and I Am with you always.
That is My promise, and I always keep My promises.
Your Shepherd, Jesus*

"Jesus told them this story: 'If a man has a hundred sheep
and one of them gets lost, what will he do?
Won't he leave the ninety-nine others in the wilderness
and go in search for the one that is lost until he finds it?
And when he has found it, he will joyfully
carry it home on his shoulders.'"
Luke 15:3–5, NLT

No More

No more lies,
No more good-byes.
No more suffering, sorrow, or pain.
No more tragedy, trauma, or calamity.
No more death.
No more night or freezing cold—
No more need for coats, hats, and boots.
And no more sun.
The Light shining from our awesome God
and His begotten Son, will be our "Sun" forevermore.
Heaven is all good and
"no one will take away your joy."
John 16:22, NIV

Visible Grief

Lord, I have spent too much time looking out from
within a glass goblet.
It's usually filled with something cold, creamy,
and drizzled with chocolate.
Yes, I admit an addiction to the sweet stuff—
It "helps" to fill the lonely, sad, painful parts of me . . .
for about . . . a minute.

No one comments, Lord. Why would they?
No one is going to ask the obvious question,
"Have you put on weight?"
That would have disaster written all over it.
But I have . . . and "weigh" too much.

There is no excuse for not taking care of my body temple.
The only thing I can say is that it is an outward sign
of my internal grief and struggles.
God, please fix it. Take the spoon out of my mouth!
You are my comfort.
Please teach me that I don't need to feed an addition,
even for a minute.
I don't want to wear my sorrow and problems.
I want those to remain on the inside between You and me.
I trust that in Your perfect timing and in Your perfect way,
You will make me whole again.

Just a Piece of Paper

Life is made up of paper.
There is an oft used phrase, "we are buried in paper."
Office desks are piled high with it; perhaps it is a legal brief,
or some couple's divorce papers,
or the IRS mailing you a delinquent notice.

Paper.
We cover our walls with it, wash our faces and counter tops with it,
clean up after baby with it . . . and throw it away.
Much paper is discarded and eventually will become part of
an overloaded landfill.
But some papers are beautiful and thoughtful . . . and treasured:
birthday cards, sympathy cards, get-well cards.
Other papers we hold onto for life: birth certificates, Social
Security cards, passports, marriage licenses.

Our family has some papers that we hold onto, but they don't
bring us tears of joy to look at them.
Instead, they stab our hearts and make them bleed.

You see, we hold what remains of our son—
his "personal effects" after his tragic death.

We have treasured pictures, cards, and mementos,
and now we have
his death certificate . . . forced upon us.
It is a piece of paper we would never choose to own
. . . and never display.

It's just paper. Or is it?
The government sure places a high priority on its value.
They require us to show it, sign it, notarize it, and pay for it.
But the recordings of marriages, births, deaths and all other jots
and tittles of our lives, stored in photo albums and journals,
are treasured because their memories bring joy and soothe
our often aching hearts.

God's Word is recorded on paper too.
It also has great value placed upon it.
But we aren't required to have it stamped or notarized to prove
who we belong to . . . and its information is free.

God knows us by name and even by the number of hairs
on our heads—great or few—
and He even has our names written on the back
of His hands (Isaiah 49:16, MSG, paraphrased).

God is hoping we read His "paper" day after day
so that we fall more deeply in love with Him every time we do.

When we leave this old earth behind, we will leave all of our
paper identity behind too.
Perhaps some people will briefly panic . . . but then smile.
God's system will beat our paper trail all to pieces.
No worries. All glory.
Thank you, Lord.

Desperate for Answers

We are desperate for answers, Lord.
We get so agonizingly desperate for Truth sometimes that we
even seek answers from the enemy
. . . from those claiming to have spoken
to the ones we have loved and lost to death.

I have read the Truth in Your Word about death, Lord,
and I choose to accept all scripture as inspired by You:

"No one remembers you when he is dead.
Who praises you from the grave?"
Psalm 6:5, NIV

"For the living know that they will die,
but the dead know nothing . . .

. . . for in the grave, where you are going, there is neither working
nor planning nor knowledge nor wisdom."
Ecclesiastes 9:5, 10, NIV

He will swallow up death forever. The Sovereign Lord will
wipe away the tears from all faces . . ."
Isaiah 25:8, NIV

Some may find it comforting to think of their precious loved
ones in heaven already . . .
watching what is going on down here on the earth below.

Some find themselves reluctant to change the child's bedroom
into a more useful room for fear of
upsetting their child who they think is keeping
an eye on them from heaven.

Others may believe their loved one has gone to heaven to be an
angel, helping God do His chores.

But Lord, how can I be comforted by such thoughts if they are
only man-made traditions and not found in Your Word?
Your conversation with Your disciples when Lazarus died
helps me to understand:

"After He had said this, He went on to tell them,

*'Our friend Lazarus has fallen asleep;
but I am going to wake him up.'*

*His disciples replied, 'Lord, if he sleeps, he will get better.'
Jesus had been speaking of his death, but His disciples thought
He meant natural sleep.
So then He told them plainly,*

*'Lazarus is dead, and for your sake I am glad I was not there,
so that you may believe . . .'"*
John 11:11–14, NIV

And then there is my favorite promise about the resurrection:

*"For since we believe that Jesus died and rose again,
even so God will also bring with Him through Jesus those
who have fallen asleep [in death].*

*For this we declare to you by the Lord's [own] word,
that we who are alive and remain until the coming of the Lord
shall in no way precede [into His presence] or have any advantage over those
who have previously fallen asleep [in Him in death].*

*For the Lord Himself will descend from heaven
with a loud cry of summons . . .
And those who have departed this life in Christ will rise first."*
1 Thessalonians 4:14–16, AMP

It is so easy for us to be confused, Lord, for our hearts and minds
are in constant overload mode with pain and turmoil . . .
besides the fact that death and destruction continues at an
alarming rate all around us every day.

We want answers . . . we need to understand what happened to
those we love . . . and had to say good-bye to.

My Children,
I Love you with an everlasting Love . . . a Love beyond your
comprehension. And why is that?

"For as the sky soars high above earth, so the way I work surpasses the way
you work, and the way I think is beyond the way you think."
Isaiah 55:9, MSG

I Am your Creator, Redeemer, Friend, and Savior.
I Loved you so much that
I could not give you up . . . even though the enemy harassed
Me continuously to do so before My death.

He insisted you were not worth the trouble, but I
had to save you from his grasp.
I would do it all over again
. . . just to have you with Me for eternity.

I will comfort you every step of your life
and yes, you can expect more trouble and hardship and death.
Sin and death go hand in hand and I cannot remove them from
the earth just yet.

There will be complete answers someday.
We will have one-on-one time in heaven, and I will answer
all your questions . . . and reunite families!
I am in the business of saving lives, not destroying them, and I will never, ever
turn My back on you.

Please search My Words.
They are written to explain, answer, comfort, cheer, and save you.
There is power in these promises if you trust in Me.
My Spirit resides in hearts that long to be filled,
and through My mighty power,
your hearts can be prepared for eternity.

Meanwhile . . . you and I will walk life's pathways together.
But start looking for Me . . . it won't be long.
See you soon.

Love always,
Jesus

Memories

Merry Sunshine

He was our firstborn, my "Merry Sunshine."
Waking up to this face was pure pleasure . . . he just oozed
charisma with his toothy, juicy grins every morning.
I'd shuffle to his crib, half asleep until I'd see that smile
. . . then my heart would melt into a puddle and wake me
up enough to sing this little ditty:

"Good morning, Merry Sunshine, why did you wake so soon?
You scare the little stars away and drive away the moon."

Then he'd really turn on the charm . . . and coo a little baby tune
along with my yawning vocals.

He's in a deep sleep now . . . resting in the grave
until Jesus comes.
And when our Lord blows that huge trumpet,
it will be loud enough to wake the dead . . . and that's exactly
what we have been waiting for!

Now that he's gone, these sweet, baby memories come wafting
back over the waves of time and I wipe away a tear . . .
and smile in spite of the pain.

How I miss him—the adult and the child.
We all miss him in our lives, but we choose to go on and live
with his memories in our hearts.
It won't be long, dear son. It won't be long.

In His Honor . . .
For the Love of the Game

My family grew up on sports.
In the early years, they had several favorites,
but as they grew older and could play together with their dad,
golf took center stage.
Now the competition was on . . .
who was going to be first to beat Dad at a round of golf?

As the years rolled by and more miles separated them,
it was a challenge to get together to play, but no surprise;
they made it a priority to do that quite often . . .
making memories and having fun in a joy they all shared.

They still play, but the loss of one that they loved is keenly felt . . .
and the reminders are there
every time they get together for a round of golf.

We are nearing the anniversary of our son's death.
A brother is coming to play in a golf tournament—a tournament
he would have been playing in too.

There will be laughter, jokes, and pats on the back for
a long drive down the fairway . . .
They will also remember and talk about the good
times and highlights of all the games they've played together,
and they will dedicate this game to the one we miss so much.

Dad is going to pay a special visit to his hometown.
He may drive down his street or even past his house.
He might even circle the place where he worked . . .

But the purpose of the trip is to buy a little white ball—
a golf ball souvenir from their favorite golf course . . .
so his brother can place it in his golf ball display case.

Perhaps to some, this may seem frivolous and certainly
a waste of fuel and time.
But memories of the one you loved and lost are never wasted.
They are cherished and extended and pressed to the heart.

It may be about the final score but more likely,
it is about the love of the game and who
you love and share it with.

I believe you'd agree, Lord.
You also love the game . . . the game of life,
where we "play" for Life Eternal.
This is a goal worth playing for and once attained,
I can imagine my family again chasing a little white ball around
but this time . . . aiming for the stars.

"I press on toward the goal to win the [supreme and heavenly]
prize to which God in Christ Jesus is calling us upward."
Philippians 3:14, AMP

Dog Tags

Loss is tough.
It's tough on parents; it's tough on siblings.
Some of us grieve outwardly to anyone who will listen.
Others of us keep our pain locked up inside.
Regardless of how we grieve, God knows how we feel.
As different as each snowflake that falls,
we are each a unique creature, formed from His hand.

Such is the uniqueness of a brother, now an only child.
He is strong, yet tender.
He is quiet, and yet thinks deeply.
He is kind and loving and he knows pain.

He lost his best friend—his brother.

We discovered his dog tag left behind after a recent visit.
It showed visible signs of wear,
having been popped on and off countless times.
It was special; a gift from a military brother.
Each son got one.

One son remains and his painful loss runs deep.
Upon closer inspection, we discovered not one, but both
dog tags fastened together, worn together.

We all remember in different ways.
Love in different ways.
Relate to God in different ways.
God knows what is on our son's heart every moment.
He knows why he wears both dog tags
and what they mean to him.

I am sure that our son and God pick quiet moments
to chat together.
God in His gentleness, knows exactly what our son needs
and whispers to his heart.
Perhaps it has nothing to do with sadness of the past,
but plans for the future.

When our family gathers in heaven above,
perhaps one brother will toss the other brother his dog tag.
But for right now, the reminder that dangles on his chest
is a way to keep his brother tucked in his heart.
And that says it all.

*"He will be careful not to cut off one bruised branch
or to blow out the flickering flame of even one candle.
In faithfulness He will bring forth justice and equity for all."*
Isaiah 42:3, Clear Word Bible

Relationships

Footprints

The Lord says, "I will guide you along the best pathway for your life.
I will advise you and watch over you."
Psalm 32:8, NLT

". . .Follow the Lamb wherever He goes . . ."
Revelation 14:4, AMP

Dear Lord,
Please leave clear footprints and I will follow them, for without
Your guidance, I will surely lose my way.
The road of life is bumpy and hilly with dangerous
drop offs everywhere.

The enemy plants ambushes in dark places, but I can
trust You to lead me to safety for
"there is a greater power with us than with him."
2 Chronicles 32:7, NCV

You know all of my footprints, Lord.
I can hide nothing from You.
You know every place I have ever been and every wrong
choice I have made.

You know my footprints of sorrow.
You know that I have fallen at Your feet many times,
begging for mercy.

Taking steps after tragedy is difficult
and often feels impossible to do.
One would rather curl up in a ball
and stay that way forever.

But You have shown me how to move forward,
leaning heavily on You for support;

in fact, You have often carried me or allowed me to walk on
Your feet like I did with my daddy when I was a little child.

But please, Lord, don't get too far ahead of me.
I must still be able to see Your footprints
ever guiding me to a better land.

Sometimes when I look up at the puffy clouds, I can imagine I
see Your footprints, drawing closer and closer to this earth.
Soon You will be within shouting distance and we will each
hear the musical sound of Your powerful voice—
calling all Your children,
those awake and those asleep.

I can almost hear You say,

"It's time children. You who are asleep, wake up!
We are going home at last!"

I can imagine Your laughter as You greet us one by one.
O, what a happy day that will be!

No more need to follow You, Lord, trailing behind and trying to
catch up to Your long strides . . . for in heaven,
these dim eyes will see You in all Your radiance and glory!
And we'll be together at last.

Embracing True Faith

". . . But I can promise you this.
If you had faith no larger than a mustard seed, you could tell this
mountain to move from here to there, and it would.
Everything would be possible for you."
Matthew 17:20, CEV

Dear God,
When the enemy killed our son,
my belief in You took a nose dive . . .
and I blamed You for his death.
But You and I have discussed this and I no longer feel that way—
and thank You again for forgiving me.

But growth upward is slow.
I feel like my faith is the size of a tiny grain of mustard seed,
so how could it ever become the size of a tree,
a tree that is large enough to provide shelter for nesting birds?

I know the enemy is angrily pacing about, trying to erect walls
to keep my trust in You from growing.
Perhaps he brings me alongside believers
who give false information—
but they are Your worshippers too, Lord.
They are Your children!
How can I sort out the true faithful from the counterfeit faithful?

My Dear Child,
The whole point of what I'm urging is simply Love—
Love uncontaminated
by self-interest and counterfeit faith; a life open to Me.
Those who fail to keep to this point soon wander off
into a cul-de-sac of gossip.

They set themselves up as experts on religious issues,
but haven't the remotest idea of what they're holding forth
with such imposing eloquence.

You have been anointed by Me from the very beginning
and that is all that matters.
I will carry you moment by moment as you lean on Me and trust in My
anointing, which is real and not counterfeit.

I have taught you the Truth in everything you need to know
about yourself and Me.
It is uncontaminated by the lies of so-called believers,
so live deeply in what I have taught you.

Let it sink into your life as you follow both Me and Dad
and your faith will grow.
It will lead to what I promised you: real life, eternal life!
1 Timothy 1:4–6; 1 John 2:24, 25, 27, MSG, *paraphrased*

The Magnetism of His Love

We are as opposite as heaven is from earth . . .
so what could possibly attract Him to us?
He was born to die; we were born to live.
He asked His Father to forgive His murderers—
we cursed Him and spit in His face.
He gives—we take, and often without thankfulness.
Our hearts beat in perfect rhythm—His gift of life.
He Loves us unconditionally—we love with strings attached.
He paid the ultimate price for sin so that we owe
nothing but love in return.
Oh, the Power of Him who Loves us with an inexhaustible Love!
His magnetism cannot be denied.
We are naturally drawn to Him—the bonds of Love are unmistakable.
What wondrous, awesome Love!
How beyond our wildest dreams!
Therefore . . .

". . . Do you think anyone is going to be able to drive a wedge
between us and Christ's love for us?
There is no way!"
Romans 8:31, MSG

It's Not About Me

It's not about me, Lord, it never has been.
But it is tough to come to grips with the fact that I am not
in charge of my life.

I am not in charge of my children's lives either.
I can control nothing but my own choices and even then,
I need all the help You can give me.

It was not until our son passed away that I realized how little
control I have.
I could not prevent his death . . . and neither could anyone else
. . . except You.

It hurts that You could have stopped his death,
but You chose not to.

I would have prevented it if I could have, so why didn't You
when Your Love is even greater than ours?

It was when I had begun to search Your Word that my eyes
fell on a verse that had never made much sense . . . until now:

*". . . just as the heavens are higher than the earth,
so My ways are higher than your ways and My thoughts
higher than your thoughts."*
Isaiah 55:9, NLT

When I read this verse, I had to bow in submission to the
One who is greater than I am.

Though I will never understand, this side of heaven, why You
chose to let my son die,
I choose to accept Your Word as Truth
and trust that You know what You are doing.

We miss him terribly and we will
until our own eyes close in death.
But you, Lord, see from beginning to end and through
the eyes of eternity.
Time on this earth is short in comparison
to the length of eternal life.

So I will continue to trust Your plan and choices, Lord.
Yes, I chose to trust in Your unfailing Love . . .
and love you back.

His Hand of Comfort

"I am the One who comforts you."
Isaiah 51:12, NLT

"God blesses those people who grieve. They will find comfort!"
Matthew 5:4, CEV

*"Praise be to the God and Father of our Lord Jesus Christ,
the Father of compassion and the God of all comfort."*
2 Corinthians 1:3, NIV

Ah, the yummy concoctions we call comfort food:
fluffy mashed potatoes and gravy, baked-to-perfection macaroni
and cheese, hot fudge sauce over mounds of home-churned
ice cream to name just a few of my favorites.
You will have to make your own list . . . that is, if you dare
to admit that you like them too!

Lord, these foods are smooth and creamy or warm and gooey,
and they slide down so effortlessly.
But the comfort goes away when the food is gone . . .
Gone, but unfortunately not forgotten since it seems to meander
down to my hips and stick there.

Thank You, Lord,
for Your warm hand of comfort on my shoulder yesterday.
Thank You for whispering soothing,
sweet peace into my ear, flooding my being like warmed honey.

Thank You for being my true comfort; my lasting comfort—
and the only One who is able to reach inside where it hurts
and tenderly hold my heart.
I love you, God.

"May I Take Your Problems?"

"But there are too many of them and besides, I am sure they are
too difficult for You to handle, Jesus," I responded.

"I can't ask or expect You to be able to fix them.
They have always been this way and probably always will be.
I pray and nothing seems to happen,
so I doubt that You can fix them,
but thanks for the offer."

"Oh, and by the way, we heard a report
that You restored sight to a blind man.
How wonderful, if it is true," I said, half under my breath.

After all, His good friend Lazarus was allowed to die.
I suspect that the healed blind man was just a hoax as well . . .
some half-baked story the media put out just to grab headlines.

But today I have come to the tomb of Lazarus out of respect for
his sisters Mary and Martha,
and also because I happen to be on assignment.
You see, I am a reporter for the *Bethany Times*.

My camera crew is with me.
We are allowed to be right up front so we can print the real story
in tomorrow's newspaper.
I expect this to be on the front page—
the "big break" I have been waiting for . . .
and perhaps it will grant me a hefty raise.

How sad the sisters must be to lose their only brother.
They, along with the hired mourners, are wailing loudly.
It makes me wonder how their friend Jesus
could fail them in their
time of greatest need.

Oh look, here He comes now.
If anything is going to happen today I won't miss it;
no foul-ups on my watch.
I will see it with my own eyes, and we will record it for the world.

Jesus looks both upset and sad; He has tears in His eyes.
Apparently, He did Love His friend a whole lot.
It looks like He's going to pray,
but He's not looking toward the temple.
Instead, He's looking up to the sky.

I must listen carefully and put the mike up close;
He's talking softly.

Thanks, Dad, for always listening to Me.
You and I have such a tight relationship that
We can discuss everything
and We often do, back and forth all day long
and all night too, sometimes.

But this request isn't for Me;
it's for those who are listening intently to
My every Word.

*They are so quick to judge Me unfairly and they
doubt Your Power through Me.*

*So I ask You, for the benefit of all those present,
to wake up Lazarus.
Perhaps, Dad, more will believe in You today
after their friend is returned to them,
and believe also that You did send Me.*
John 11:33–43, MSG, paraphrased

And then He shouted at the cave for Lazarus to come out . . .
and he did!
Unbelievable! Magnificent!

And there you have it, folks.
We have all witnessed Jesus Christ's awesome power today,
and we can't help but believe what our eyes have seen!

I can now say without a doubt that I can trust Him
to handle all of my problems.
I hope He asks me again if He can help, and when He does,
I shall answer, "Yes!"

Awesome God!

God spoke the worlds and everything in them into existence
and keeps them in perfect balance
with the tips of His giant fingers.

He made the liquid ball of sun to heat the day and the dew drop
of moon to give us light at night.
He tossed diamonds in the velvety, night sky to twinkle
and blink their wonder.

The God who makes rain fall and parted the waters,
exposing dry land for Israelite feet,
must care a great deal about our comfort and needs.
Can I trust in His unfailing Love and goodness?

Yes, I can.
Thank you, God.
Words fail me to express how I feel about You.
But You are indeed Awesome!

Daily Chat

Dear Jesus,
You and I have been chatting back and forth
for a long time, now.
Perhaps I should clarify that a bit . . .
I do most of the talking while You listen.

I have told You over and over that I want to be
more like You.
I desire to share the same
close relationship You have with Your Father.
You have told me that it is possible, but I first must
let go of everything and give it to you.
I must trust You completely . . .instead of hashing and rehashing
each day's events and concerns.

Am I supposed to say something like,
"Jesus, You already know all my problems today,
so I am asking You to handle them.
Thanks!"

But that sounds too simple—way too easy.
Are You sure there isn't more I need to do or say first?

"No, My Child," He answers kindly. *"I Am*
the same yesterday, today, and forever.
You can trust Me with all your heart and lean on Me for understanding.
I've got your back . . . and front.
Now all I need is permission to have all of your heart."

Love,
Jesus

Hebrews 13:8; Proverbs 3:5, NIV, paraphrased

Build on the Rock

My Child,
You must listen to My Words in order to heed their teachings.
And if you do, you will be like the wise person
who built his house
on a firm foundation by digging down deeply into solid rock.
He is prepared when the floodwaters rise and
break against the house. It will stand firm.
Luke 6:48, NLT, paraphrased

On the other hand, if you just read My Words and don't
work them into your daily life, you are like
the stupid carpenter who builds his house on a sandy beach.
When a storm rolls in and the waves come up,
it will collapse like a deck of cards.
Matthew 7:26–27, MSG, paraphrased

Consider the first house with a firm foundation.
This person reads and heeds My Words, sweeping his new
house clean of all evil.
It is kept clean and tidy . . . but empty.
The enemy keeps watch.
He will return to that same home and bring more demons with him

and the condition of this man's heart will be worse
than if he had never built it on a firm foundation in the first place.
Matthew 12:43–45, NIV, paraphrased

You see, My Child, I know the condition of your "house."
I know when it is swept clean but remains empty.
And I long to fill it with My Love and power,
but you must first let Me in.

". . . I stand at the door and knock . . ."
Revelation 3:20, NIV

I won't barge in against your will, but the enemy will.
He'll peek in the windows and if he sees
that your house remains empty,
he'll return and force his way in with many demons in tow
in his attempt to completely destroy you.

Please, let Me in. Let's study and learn together.
Let's put your firm foundation to good use.
Let Me save you from destruction.

Your Friend,
Jesus

Now I Lay Me Down to Sleep

"I found myself in trouble and went looking for my Lord; my life
was an open wound that wouldn't heal.
When friends said, 'Everything will turn out alright.'
I didn't believe a word they said.
I remember God—and shake my head.
I bow my head—then wring my hands.
I'm awake all night—not a wink of sleep; I can't even say
what's bothering me.
I go over the days one by one. I ponder the years gone by."
Psalm 77:2–5, MSG

I am tired and worn, Lord.
The days are long and often feel pointless—
and the nights drag on even longer, especially if sleep won't come.
My mind replays sad moments or lines up the next day's
activities, and it is hard to shut it off, so I ask
You to take my thoughts captive
and give me Your perfect
peace and sweet sleep.

Love You,
Amen

2 Corinthians 10:5, NIV; Isaiah 26:3, NIV; Proverbs 3:24, NIV,
paraphrased

Untamed Fears

Dear Lord,
Why do I, at times, still shudder in uncontrollable fear?
It's as if frightening, childhood memories still control me. Why?
I don't get it.

I have You to shelter me from the howling winds
and raging storms
so why would I still be afraid?
Lord, there must be more to this fear thing than
I understand.

Please teach me to trust in You until there is no longer
the tiniest particle of fear remaining in me.

Love You,
Amen.

Psalm 55:8, CEV, paraphrased

God "in a Box"

"But, God, can You really live here on the earth?
The sky and the highest place in heaven cannot contain You.
Surely this house which I have built cannot contain You."
1 Kings 8:27, NCV

I was thinking about an old toy, Lord.
One that I used to play with when I was a child,
and then we bought one for our children. Remember?

It was a box that played a tune and then
burst open and up popped a clown or some other cute surprise.
It was startling the first time;
then I, like all children before and after me,
played it over and over again—
driving mine and generations of parents crazy.

Using the toy as an analogy, perhaps that is how I viewed You
when I was a child growing up.
You were like that toy—easily contained in a box that
sat on a shelf or lay forgotten at the bottom of my toy chest.

You might be pulled out to be played with once in awhile—
pop up, get a reaction, and then Your lid would be slammed down
and You would be out of sight until the next whim.

How sad to think You were nothing more than a
"God-in-a-box" toy to me.
From a childish viewpoint, You were not needed very often,
and You couldn't be very powerful;
after all, You fit in a pint-sized box.

That was then, but how about now?
Have I let You out of Your "box" yet?
Have I begun to realize how mammoth You really are,
and that You could never be contained on any scale?

In Job 37, MSG, one of Job's friends confronts him:

*"Stop in your tracks! Take in God's miracle-wonders!
Do you have any idea how God does it all,
How He makes bright lightning from dark storms,
how He piles up the cumulus clouds—all these
miracle-wonders of a perfect Mind?"*

*"Mighty God! Far beyond our reach! Unsurpassable in
power and justice!
It's unthinkable that He'd treat anyone unfairly. So bow to Him
in deep reverence, one and all!
If you're wise, you'll most certainly worship Him."*

Then God confronts Job in chapter 38, MSG:

*"I have some questions for you,
and I want some straight answers.
Where were you when I created the earth?
Who decided on its size? Certainly you'll know that!
Who came up with the blueprints and measurements?
How was its foundation poured and who set the cornerstone,
while the morning stars sang in chorus and all the angels
shouted praise?*

*And who took charge of the ocean
when it gushed forth like a baby from the womb?
That was Me! I wrapped it in soft clouds and
tucked it in safely at night.*

*Do you know where Light comes from
and where Darkness lives
So you can take them by the hand and lead them
home when they get lost?
Have you ever traveled to where snow is made,
seen the vault where hail is stockpiled,
the arsenals of hail and snow that I keep in readiness
for times of battle and war?"*

God raised one challenging question after another and
volleyed them one by one at Job. Bull's-eye.
Job had no response. How could he?
Our God is an awesome, majestic, and powerful God!

"O Lord, there is none like You, nor is there any God beside You,
according to all that our ears have heard."
1 Chronicles 17:20, AMP

You cannot be contained . . . not in a box,
nor in a structure of any kind, and I am so grateful.

Thank You, God.

Fresh Faithfulness

"Because of the Lord's great love we are not consumed,
for His compassions never fail. They are new every morning;
great is Your faithfulness."
Lamentations 3:22–23, NIV

"When life is heavy and hard to take, go off by yourself.
Enter the silence. Bow in prayer. Don't ask questions: wait for hope to appear."
Lamentations 3:28–29, MSG

Heavenly Father,
What promises fill the pages of Your precious Word.
Waiting for the blessed hope . . . the longing for Your return.
And yet, You say to occupy until You come.

I know that I am to occupy in such a way that brings glory to
Your name and prayerfully show others
what a tender, loving God You are.
Thank You for saving us . . . already.

Thank You for preparing mansions all over heaven for us, Your kids.

Life gets heavy.
Waiting is hard.

The longing to have our family reunited again grows
and pulls at my heart
with deeper intensity every day.

But each new day also brings fresh hope, fresh compassion,
and fresh comfort from Your heart to mine.

Thank You, Father, for Your fresh bounty
of faithfulness.

The Eye of the Storm

"Be still, and know that I Am God; I will be exalted among the nations, I will be
exalted in the earth."
Psalm 46:10, NIV

Peace be still . . .

"But soon a fierce storm came up.
High waves were breaking into the boat, and it began to fill with water. Jesus
was sleeping at the back of the boat with
His head on a cushion.

The disciples woke Him up, shouting,
'Teacher, don't You care that we're going to drown?'

When Jesus woke up, He rebuked the wind and said to the waves,
'Silence! Be still!'

Suddenly the wind stopped, and there was a great calm.
Then He asked them, 'Why are you afraid?
Do you still have no faith?'"

. . . and know that I Am God.

"The disciples were absolutely terrified.
'Who is this man?' they asked each other.
'Even the wind and waves obey Him!'"
Mark 4:37–41, NLT

Dear Jesus,
This story is filled with deep meaning for me.
How many times have I been caught in the storms of life,
struggling to bail myself out without thinking
to call on You for help?

You can ask me the same questions because they apply.

Why are you afraid?
Do you still have no faith?

Apparently, Your disciples already had opportunity
for their tiny faith to be tested and grown,
but You said they had "no" faith
. . . even after witnessing Your miracles.

Jesus, please lift me up during the treacherous storms of pain
and suffering that continue to assail me.
Please guide me to safety and then teach me more about trusting
in You so that my faith may grow.

You are the only One who speaks to nature and it obeys.
You are the only One who I want to speak to
my heart and have it obey.

And like Your disciples, I too stand in awe.

Through Your Eyes

Dear Lord,
Let me see the beauty You have created through Your
eyes instead of mine.
My eyes are dim from maturity and often veiled from Truth . . .
and because they are, I often give voice to complaints
about Your other children.

Please let me see others as You see them . . .
through Your perfect vision.
It's because of grace, isn't it . . . that we have eyes to see at all?

Oh, what perfect grace and beauty we have in Jesus . . .
how blessed we are to belong, really belong.
And because we belong . . . we have an urgent mission.

*"We proclaim Him, admonishing every man and
teaching every man with all wisdom,
so that we may present every man complete in Christ."*
Colossians 1:28, NASB

Only You can complete me, Lord.
Thank You.

Lean on Me

My Child,

*When the storms of life are threatening,
Lean on Me.*

*When you can't see where you're going with your eyes brimming with tears,
Lean on me.*

When your back is tired and the sink is full of dirty dishes,
Lean on Me.

When the children are whining and pushing your buttons,
Lean on Me.

And when the devil pushes your buttons,
Lean on Me.

When trouble strikes and you've nowhere to turn,
Lean on Me.

When the creditors call and threaten you,
Lean on Me.

Have you figured it out yet, My Child?

I Am
All you need for all the situations you will ever face
every breathing moment of your life.

I Am

your Loving, Almighty, Everlasting, All-powerful God—
your Tower of Strength when you have none.
Your hiding place while the lightning flashes and the thunder rolls.
Your soft, gentle words of comfort when your heart is breaking with sadness.

So . . .

lean on My Everlasting Arms where you will be
safe and snug, warm and dry.
I Love you, I Love you, I Love you,
My cherished one.
You are Mine and I will never, ever give you up.

—God

"It Is Finished"

We might say these three words together on occasion
without giving them much thought.
They simply mean an end to something—
like a meal or a golf tournament or a complicated surgery.
And then we move on; nothing significant.

But when Jesus uttered these three words on the cross—
and then died—
everything changed.

His earthly mission was finished . . .
no more innocent lambs need be slain.
Satan lost the war and in time,
he would die eternally.

Because Jesus said, "It is finished" (John 19:30, NIV)
and gave up His breath,
we have a one-of-a-kind gift available for the choosing
with no strings attached.
Jesus gives us the promise of life everlasting because of His
everlasting Love.

These three, priceless words are meant for us to remember and
savor;
and above all, to make a personal promise to the
One who died for us—
I want to be there to greet you . . .
and start a new beginning in heaven.
Agreed?

My Gardener God

". . . let our gardener, God, landscape you with the Word, making
a salvation-garden of your life."
James 1:21, MSG

Lord, I loved this text so much that I am "borrowing" it
for our conversation together.
What a concept—You as my Gardener!
I love it . . . and I love a beautiful garden, but unfortunately,
I was not born with a green thumb and
many years of practice doesn't seem to have changed that much.

So I am looking forward to my heavenly garden where there
will be no blight of any kind: no bind weed, no ticks, no
leaf-crunching beetles or thirsty mosquitoes.
The list is endless, but You get the idea.

I will contentedly play in the dark, moist, humus-rich soil all day long
without the slightest fear of scorching sunburn or biting flies . . .
and perhaps no sweat either?
I can dream, can't I?

Ah, the exquisite fragrance of a delicate rose . . . and in heaven
there will be no sharp thorns to spoil my enjoyment.
The lilac bushes with their heady fragrance,
tulip trees blanketed with fragile
blossoms, and Shasta daisies covered in happy smiles.
I am eager and ready, Lord, to take it all in.

You will be my personal Gardener and we will have
wonderful times together.
Just think of all the details You can share with me
. . . how You designed
the perfect acorn squash, beefsteak tomato,
and yellow sweet corn. Yum!

I will remember every tip and apply them to my acreage.
Yes, I said acreage . . . no need to till . . . no weeds, ever!
And just think I will never get tired working my large estate!

A perfect garden is just one more reason to look forward
to Your soon return.
I am ready to hang up my hat, toss the gloves and insect spray,
and prepare for the time of my eternal life.

But based on the text above, I think that
You have a different garden in mind—
a garden of the heart.
I have trouble with that one too, Lord.
I get tangled up in the weeds of sin and I struggle
with the fruits of the Spirit.

I am asking You to make a salvation garden in my heart, God.
You are so multi-talented that I don't have to worry
about the plans or outcome.
I choose to surrender my future landscape and
the landscape of my heart
to You right now, every moment of every day.
I will let You take charge of planting good seed in Your special
soil in my heart and watch me bloom for Your glory.
Thank you, my Gardener God.

In My Grip

My Child,
Even though the way seems rough and uncertain,
I have picked you up and I will never drop you.
There is no need to fear, for I Am Your God.
I will strengthen you, help you, and hold you steady when
turbulence threatens to overturn you.
You are in My grip.

*There are days when you probably feel like the enemy is at your
back and hemming you in on all sides.
But you can't see like I can.
I have surrounded you with scores of holy, warring angels
who will fight the adversary if he threatens you, but he won't.*

*He runs from My power. He is no match for Me.
So do not worry about the enemy.
I am right here and I am not letting go.*

*Still not convinced?
How about the poor and thirsting who are desperate for water?
I will open up rivers for them on the barren hills and spout
fountains in the valleys.
I will turn the baked-clay badlands into a cool pond and the
waterless waste into splashing creeks.*

*And not only that, I will plant the red cedar in the treeless wasteland,
also acacia, myrtle, and the olive tree.
I'll place the cypress in the desert with plenty of oaks and pines.*

*No one will miss this.
It will be the unavoidable, indisputable evidence that I, God,
will personally take care of your needs.
It's created and signed in My handwriting.
No matter what it takes, I have thousands of ways to provide for your needs.*

*Now are you convinced?
You can trust in Me.
I Am your Forever God and I Am in Love with you.*
Isaiah 41, MSG, paraphrased

Soaking You Up

Father God,
This might sound silly to some people, but You already know
that I love to soak in a tub of hot water, and yes . . .
a plethora of bubbles is nice too.

Add a scented candle with its soft glow and lovely fragrance . . .
and You and I can settle in to enjoy some thoughtful,
quiet moments together.

Of course, we must allow room in this tranquil setting
for the family cat
who loves to swipe his paw in the hot water and lick it dry.
Not my taste, but apparently he enjoys it.

Soaking up Your Word is equally as lovely
when I dwell on verses of
scripture that quiet my aching heart and
soothe my troubled spirit.

You know what I am referring to, Lord.
Our son passed away a few years ago and his absence is
keenly felt in our family.
The death of a child causes gut-wrenching, gnawing pain.

What would I ever do without You to console me when tears
threaten to carry me away like a swollen river?
Thank You, gracious Father, for collecting my tears
in Your bottle—
just like You keep track of the hairs on my head.
With that kind of counting,
You show such tender regard for every inch of me.

"Though I walk through the [deep, sunless] valley of the shadow of death,
I will fear or dread no evil, for You are with me;
Your rod [to protect] and Your staff [to guide],
they comfort me."
Psalm 23:4, AMP

I'm Falling in Love Again

Ours was a casual, on-again and off-again relationship.
I inherited Christian duty from my parents.
I obeyed, attended church faithfully, and studied the Bible
to make good grades.
It all had a sensible ring to it, but it was shallow and unfulfilling.

Not until I was on my own did I realize that I needed more.
But time marched on as I gained a husband and family
and all the busyness of life.
We were complete, all of us together.
Life was good.

I tried to be a loving, responsible mother.
My children would always be safe on my watch.
Their needs came before mine, always.
They grew into adulthood and left our nest empty,
which took some getting used to . . .
and not without some tears along the way.

It never occurred to me that I might be forced
to give one of them up . . .
a seed I grew in my belly that I watched develop into manhood.
Who would demand such a thing?

Oh, there were the car-accident worries every parent has that
comes as an attachment to a teen's driver's license.

But when nothing happened within the first few months,
I dared to let out a sigh of relief.

So nothing, absolutely nothing could have prepared me
for the unthinkable.
Never would I have thought about suicide.
Never.

But it happened and it changed all of us forever.
It was a life-changing trauma—a horrific tragedy with absolute
crushing, heart-smashing pain.

I have written descriptive words before, but there are always
more, and more, and still more.
I was too mute, too wasted, and in too much throbbing pain to
wonder where God was in all of this.

I hadn't really wondered seriously about our relationship . . .
I assumed we had one and it was okay.
But suddenly, I hated God.
I hated Him with all the rage within the core of my being.
How dare He take my child!
How dare He let such a thing happen when He had all the power
to stop him, but He didn't. Why not?
WHY NOT??

No answers. Only questions.
We could query the vastness of the Internet all we wanted, but
we would never have answers.
There were none.

It took time before I began to realize that God had never left
me or my family alone.
No matter how long the tunnel of grief,

He will walk by our sides—
holding our hands, arms around our shoulders,
carrying us mile after mile if need be and always whispering
His promises in our ears:

My Children,
Behold I come quickly and every eye shall see Me . . .
Revelation 1:7, AMP, paraphrased

Every eye, and that means your whole family, including the ones
who have been asleep.
Hold on . . . hold on.

Yes, Lord, I will hold on to You and all Your precious promises.
You are teaching me day by day and I am,
perhaps for the first time ever—
truly falling in love with You.

Yip Yap

That's not his real name, but that's what I call him.
He's not ours; he belongs to the neighbors.
Every day when it's fresh air time, he barks continuously . . .
and I mean he doesn't pause for a second.

He's as cute as a button with a scruffy coat and
a wagging tail . . . but the bark!
I close up the windows or turn on some noise to try
to drown him out.
How can I even concentrate enough to write!

Lord, there has to be a lesson here somewhere, even though
I'd rather muzzle Yip Yap.

Perhaps it is this: life is full of disturbances and distractions
that take up our time.

Sometimes they are just noise and serve no purpose.
But often they are calculated noises planted by the enemy to keep
us occupied with ourselves; leaving little time to build a
relationship with You.

No matter what, Lord, You come first so please restore
my soul in spite of the "yip yaps" of life.

"If I could speak all the languages of earth and of angels,
but didn't love others, I would only be
a noisy gong or a clanging cymbal."
1 Corinthians 13:1, NLT

In the Nick of Time

"Then, in your desperate condition, you called out to God.
He got you out in the nick of time; He put your feet on a wonderful road that took
you straight to a good place to live.
So thank God for His marvelous love,
for His miracle mercy to the children He loves."
Psalm 107:4, MSG

"You have melanoma," she had said.
Those are such alarming words, Lord.
In spite of her soft tone,
I felt like I had been punched in the stomach.
Hearing that phrase was not on my "to do" list today,
but it was on Yours.

I got the good news/bad news approach.
But it really was all good news.

Thanks to You, my thoughtful God, it was caught
in the nick of time!

I am so grateful that You set up circumstances
so that what I thought to be a harmless mole
caught the eye of a specialist friend.
And because of her training, it's all good news!

We usually say, "It was luck" or some other such phrase.
But You are teaching me that there is no such thing as "luck."
You are sometimes loud, but more often You are subtly working
things out for our good (Romans 8:28, NIV),
whether we give You the credit or not.

Therefore, I am proclaiming for all to read . . .
You save Your children to the uttermost.
You always have our best interest at heart.
You created us, Love us passionately, gave up Your life for us,
and You have our mansions in heaven ready and waiting
for us to move into.

So thank You for small moles requiring only a few stitches
and a bit of discomfort.
Whatever it takes, Lord, we are in this thing together.
You and me . . . "buds" for all eternity.

"God, pick up the pieces, put me back together again.
You are my praise!"
Jeremiah 17:14, MSG

The Blame Game

*"The man said, 'You gave this woman to me and she gave me
fruit from the tree, so I ate it.'"*
Genesis 3:12, NCV

We live in a world of blame, Lord.
Over and over again it is someone else's fault, and not ours.

Perhaps the blame game began in heaven with Lucifer
since sin originated with him.
But the first recorded story in the Bible
centered on Adam and Eve . . .
and I know I don't have to remind You about them.
The first spat began with our first parents in the garden when
Adam essentially blamed You for
giving him a woman who led him astray!
It may be an old story, but it is a familiar and current problem.

Even today on the news, someone political had been unfaithful.
"But why blame me?" he whines.
"There was another politician who did the same thing weeks ago
and nobody went after him!"

Around and around it goes . . . no one wants to take a stand and
say the tough, but simple words, "I alone, am responsible."

Lord, help me not to blame others for my sins.
We all have sinned . . .
but other folks' sins are Your problem, not mine.

Please Lord, I desire Your Truth in my inward parts—deep in
my heart where only You dwell. Amen.

*"Who put wisdom inside the mind
or understanding in the heart?"*
Job 38:36, NCV

Could This Be Why?

Week after week, church service after church service,
we sing our hymns to You in such a monotone
and virtually void of enthusiasm.
This baffles me. Does it baffle You, God?
Could it be that our hearts have nothing to sing about?

For "what you say flows from what is in your heart."
Luke 6:45, NLT

If there is no abundance, is there no praise?
And if there is no praise, is there no joy?
Could it be that a heart that has not been exercised
in faith and trust through difficult circumstances
is a heart unable to fully rejoice in the blessings of God?

A Prayer for Lost Sheep

"Ask the Lord for rain in the springtime;
it is the Lord who makes the storm clouds.
He gives showers of rain to men, and plants of the field to everyone.
The idols speak deceit, diviners see visions that lie,
they tell dreams that are false, they give comfort in vain.
Therefore the people wander like sheep, oppressed for lack of a shepherd."
Zechariah 10:1–2, NIV

Sheep, Lord.
We are just a bunch of dumb sheep—stubborn, near-sighted, and
never looking farther ahead than the fluffy tail
of the nearest sheep . . .
and then doing as they do, not as You ask.

Lord, please make us willing to follow the path
You have charted for us.
If we would totally deny self and follow You,
we would readily agree
that we couldn't have made a better choice.

You know us best. We know us least.

You Love with such longing,
such wonderful eternal plans and hopes.
But we are more willing to love those who love us back.

". . . Look! The Lamb of God,
who takes away the sin of the world!"
John 1:29, NLT

It took a lamb, and not just any lamb, but the Lamb of God
to bridge the abyss between us sheep and heaven.

We no longer need to follow the "tail" in front of us.
Instead, we can choose to follow the footsteps of our
best Friend and Redeemer.

". . . and they follow the Lamb wherever He leads.
They have been rescued to be presented to God and the Lamb as the most
precious people on earth."
Revelation 14:4, CEV

Lukewarm

Lukewarm is not my favorite temperature.
I don't care if it is lukewarm water or lukewarm food
or lukewarm soda pop;
it is likely to be spit out.

And nothing gives a poor first impression like a limp handshake.

It doesn't sound like God cares for lukewarm either:

". . . Because you are lukewarm—neither hot nor cold—
I am about to spit you out of My mouth."
Revelation 3:16, NIV

Jesus is speaking to His end-time church, which is our
present generation of believers.
And there is no time like the present to warm up,
in fact, to get on fire for Him.

Jesus is seeking those who choose to overcome—
those who realize they are poor, wretched, blind, and naked
and in need of a Savior.
Their eyes have been opened and they can no longer say that they
are self-sufficient and in need of nothing.

How much better to be hot and on fire for the Living God
and an overcomer by His power!
Then we have a fresh, vibrant testimony to share with others.
Sitting on a heavenly throne, reigning with Jesus Christ
beats lukewarm . . . anytime!

Your Last Day

If it were your last day on earth, how would you spend your time?
What would be important to you?
Life would become instantly serious, wouldn't it?
Suddenly, the trivial pursuits of
bank accounts, stock market values, the latest gossip—
all would cease to be important, wouldn't they?

Would you hug your children extra tight
and tell them you love them?
Would you stay on your knees longer in prayer?
Would you seek forgiveness from those you know
you have wronged?
Would you spend the day caring for the homeless or the sick?
Or would you take one last opportunity
to write to your congressman about the errors in government?
Would you bother to make out a "to do" list or
count your money in the bank one last time, or withdraw it all?
Would you smile more? Love more? Pray more?
Would you take one last walk in nature, God's second book?

Life is fleeting.
Tomorrow has not been promised.
Perhaps today is the day to plan for eternity.

*"Since everything here today might well be gone tomorrow,
do you see how essential it is to live a holy life?"*
2 Peter 3:11, MSG

"It pays to take life seriously; things work out when you trust in God."
Proverbs 16:20, MSG

Do You Miss Me?

*My Dear Wife-To-Be,
I miss you so much that My heart feels raw.
Do you miss Me too?*

*Our long-distance relationship stinks, doesn't it?
I long for a change. I long for us to be united and live in the
same place together forever.*

105

I haven't heard from you for a while.
Perhaps you are too busy to write.
I save your phone messages and listen to them over and over.
Somehow that comforts My heart, but I long for more.

I hope that you aren't getting "cold feet."
We have already changed the date once—
You're not thinking about putting our wedding day
off again, are you?
Please don't do that.
No matter what anyone else is telling you, we are meant to be together.
Don't you see that?

We are a perfect blend and life will be so much better
after we are married.
I Love you with all My heart . . . do you still love Me?

Absence could make your heart grow fonder for someone else,
but I hope and pray not.
If you tell Me that our engagement is off—that news will break
My heart forever.

Please write or call or get in touch with Me in some way.
I need to know what is on your mind;
what you think about . . . and if you ever think about Me.
Time passes so slowly without you.
But you are planted so deep in My heart that you
will always be there.

My Love for you exceeds eternity.
You are My friend, My lover, and hopefully, soon to be My bride.

Love,
Your Husband-To-Be

*". . . You will be called the People God Loves, and your land will be called
the Bride of God, because the Lord loves you.
And your land will belong to Him as a bride belongs to her husband.*

*As a young man marries a woman, so your children will marry your land.
As a man rejoices over his new wife,
so your God will rejoice over you."*
Isaiah 62:4–5, NCV

*"Then I saw New Jerusalem, that holy city, coming down from God in heaven.
It was like a bride dressed in her wedding gown
and ready to meet her husband."*
Revelation 21:2, CEV

Wrap-Around Love

Dear Lord,
I am absolutely overwhelmed by Your Love today.
There have been no rainbows or pots of gold,
just a deep sense of Your abiding Presence.

The way gets rocky, steep, and slippery
and I am always in need of Your gentle hand.
You are always there to lift me up to higher ground with a kind
word and a pat on the back.

Lord, I am such a mixture of love and pain all at the same time . . .
most of the time.
How do I separate the two?
How do I define the love I feel for You?
You have personally touched my life in so many ways—
and probably there are many more times when I did not even
realize You were there.

So this is my bumbling attempt to say "I love You."
I love You for dying just for me.
I love You for breaking through the tomb and
showing us how You plan to break open all the tombs of Your
precious children You died to save.

I love You for being there when I need You.
I love You for never forsaking me.
I love You for showing me how to live in Your precious Word.
The list is endless, Lord,
But we will have all of eternity to finish it.
And then we will have just begun.

All Glory and Honor goes to You, my Savior and my King,
Who is Wrap-Around Love.

"Sold"

Real estate does not come cheap these days and we pay a
hefty price to own a small piece of dirt.

This earth is a part of God's real estate.
He owns our world and thousands more—
as our knowledge of the cosmos continues to unfold.

Satan does not own planet Earth . . .
even though he operates as if he does.
The most he can claim is temporary housing and
mismanagement.

However, there is still room for rejoicing.
We may have difficulty with the housing market and mortgages,
but victory is soon to be ours.
God is going to claim planet Earth as His own once again!

When He comes with all of heaven to wake up His sleeping
children with a blast of His trumpet,
He will hammer a "Sold" sign on this earth, put the devil and his
evil angels in lock up,
and take us home to heaven.

No more need to buy dirt . . . heaven's dirt is free.
Everything will be ours with nothing to buy or sell ever again.
So begin dreaming about the design of your country home with
its beautiful gardens and vineyards . . . and toss the budget.
It's all been promised by our Heavenly Real Estate Agent
and it's free.

*"But in keeping with His promise
we are looking forward to a new heaven . . ."*
2 Peter 3:13, NIV

My Father's Approval

She was a fragile child with flaxen hair, large blue eyes, and a smile
that could melt your heart from fifty paces.

There is no doubt she stole his heart the first time her tiny fingers
grasped his big one.
But in his strong, quiet way, he wasn't
given to praise.

She is a lady now with lofty goals, which include meeting the
man of her dreams, and she does.
She meets a strong, silent type . . . they soon marry
and have children.

Life is a non-stop merry-go-round.
Still, in the midst of life's hectic journey,

she looks to him for approval;
always hoping for a sweet word or two . . .
or just a smile to let her know that he approves of the way
she keeps their castle and family together.
But rarely does validation come.

If she were a concert pianist, praise from an appreciative audience
would mean little
unless her teacher or mentor first gave his approval.
Slowly, God is helping her understand that it is His approval
she so deeply desires . . .
and He assures her that she has it.
In fact, she has always had it.
After all, she is His daughter, His prize, His princess!

Long before this little one was ever born,
God already couldn't contain His joy.
Oh how He anticipated her birth!
He always had a special smile—a wink perhaps—just for her.
He adored this fair-haired child.

He Loved the young graduate with all her plans.
He presided at her wedding and was present at the birth
of each, sweet child.
He has Loved her passionately all along.
And He still does.

Even if she were to play Chopsticks on the Grand Steinway at
Carnegie Hall, He couldn't be more pleased.
She'd steal a glance in His direction and He'd wink back . . .
and give her the "thumbs up" sign.

Ah, the sweet comfort and pleasure of approval
from the Man who matters most.

My Dear Child,
Never forget, I Am forever in Love with you!
You are My precious daughter and I respect, admire, Love, and adore you!
I can't wait to embrace you and all the rest of My many
beautiful daughters and handsome sons when I welcome
each of you home at last!
Love,
God

"And I will be your Father, and you will be My sons and daughters,
says the Lord Almighty."
2 Corinthians 6:18, NLT

Death to Doubt

"Who do people think is the greatest, a person who is served or one who serves?
Isn't it the one who is served?
But I have been with you as a servant."
Luke 22:27, CEV

Dear Lord,
You are my King and Servant, Creator and Redeemer,
and Precious Friend.
How awesome You are!

You who carved out the mountain peaks
with Your powerful finger
also gently pressed adorable dimples into sweet, baby cheeks.

Those same gentle hands took a towel,
knelt before His proud, arguing disciples, and washed
their dusty, calloused feet.

The King of Kings and Lord of Lords not only hugged children

111

to His breast in warm embraces,
but hung suspended between heaven and earth to save
a dying world . . . of people like you and me.

Oh Lord, humble me, forgive me, save me.
I have harbored secret blame.
I was knocked to the floor by tragic news of excruciating loss.
And after months upon months of weeping in Your patient,
loving arms, how could I still blame You?
The God who shaped perfection out of dust and then blew His
majestic breath to fill up Adam's lungs,
still humbled Himself and took my doubt to the cross—
nailing it there.

I don't want it back . . . ever.
Like Peter, Lord, I need You to not only wash my feet,
but my hands and head . . . and my heart.
John 13:8–9, NIV, paraphrased

Thank You for remembering that I am made of dust.
Thank You for a daily scrubbing to wash some of that dust off.
Thank You for restoring my son to me . . . soon, very soon.
No more dirt naps.
And no more doubt and shame.

All glory goes to You, My Savior—
the One who is worthy of all praise.
By Your mighty power and grace we have death to the enemy!
Death to doubt!

In Reckless Abandon

When Simon Peter realized it was Jesus, he left his buddies
to work the fishing nets and dove into the sea.
John 21:7, MSG, paraphrased

Peter couldn't wait for the boat to be rowed to shore
where His Master stood.
In reckless abandon, he dove into the water
and headed for shore.
No thought of his clothing, hair and makeup (from a female
viewpoint) or whether he could swim in the frigid, choppy waves.
He had only one thought on his mind . . . he dropped everything
to see His Master—his best Friend.
Is that what it takes, Lord?
Absolute, earnest, utter, even reckless abandonment of self . . .
to drop at Your feet in complete and total surrender of my will?
You mean I have to give up everything?

This is not about my emotions or circumstances or surroundings.
This is about looking eyeball to eyeball—Creator to created—and
finally realizing there is nothing, positively nothing,
I value more than being Yours.

I have a desperate need and only You can fill it.
So give me the courage to dive headlong toward You.
Help me keep my eyes on You, stroke by stroke, until I stand
before You, dripping, breathless, but ecstatic.
Take my will Lord. It's Yours.

Love,
Your Daughter

My Dear Daughter,
Of all My disciples, Peter was the most impetuous.
He could make me laugh until My sides hurt!
But he grew up from his impetuous and self-centered nature to
total abandonment in his love for Me.

I see you standing before Me dripping wet, but your eyes bright
with excitement and love.
This world is harsh and often brutal with temptations,
so do not take your eyes off Me.
In My power and strength, I will guide you
to where I Am.

Love You,
Jesus

More "Bread" Please

"I am the Bread of Life.
The person who aligns with Me hungers no more
and thirsts no more, ever.
I have told you this explicitly because even though
you have seen Me in action,
You don't really believe Me.
Every person the Father gives Me eventually comes
comes running to Me.
And once that person is with Me, I hold on
and don't let go.
I came down from heaven not to follow My own whim,
but to accomplish the will of the
One who sent Me . . .

This is what My Father wants: that anyone who sees the Son
and trusts who He is and what He does and then aligns
with Him will enter real, eternal life . . ."
Love,
Jesus

John 6:35–39, MSG

Falling Unto Mercy

Loving Father,
I have probably called to You for mercy
more in the last few years
since we lost our son
than all the other years put together.

I don't think that I really understood what it was either . . .
but now I do . . . and oh how I need it.

Webster defines "mercy" with such words as:
refrain from doing harm,
forgiveness, kindness, or blessing—
but nothing defines mercy better than all the promises that can be
mined throughout Your Word.
Each one is rich with meaning and eloquently stated:

"But I have trusted, leaned on, and been confident in Your mercy and loving-
kindness; my heart shall rejoice and be in high spirits in Your salvation."
Psalm 13:5, AMP

"God Most High, have pity on me! Have mercy.
I run to You for safety.
In the shadow of Your wings, I seek protection till danger dies down."
Psalm 57:1–3, CEV

"My eyes are blinded by my tears.
Each day I beg for Your help,
O Lord; I lift my hands to You for mercy."
Psalm 88:9, NLT

"For the mountains may move and the hills disappear, but even then
My faithful love for you will remain.
My covenant of blessing will never be broken,
says the Lord, who has mercy on you."
Isaiah 54:10, NLT

"O give thanks to the Lord, for He is good;
for His mercy and loving-kindness endure forever!"
1 Chronicles 16:34, AMP

There are many more meaningful "mercies" to be mined
from Your Word, Father.
I had a hard time narrowing down my favorites, for each one is
rich in value and provides a "heavenly quilt" of balmy comfort.
Thank You.

I Must Come

Dear God,
Undeserving, sinful, worn and beaten up by life,
but still I must come.

I bow before You on the fringes of Your wondrous Light
and wait . . .

Will You extend Your circle of Light and draw me in?
Will You beckon me to Your throne?

You are so high and lifted up, My Father,
so holy, so magnificent, so divine.

How can I find words to express my great love once I get there?

All I will want to do is look into Your lovely face
and weep.
Weep for all the trash that I lingered over and savored
far too long.
It was all for naught.

Trifles are nothing—they don't even register on the radar screen
in the face of tragedy or adversity.
Those of us who have been struck down by such horrors
are in agreement about one thing:
we no longer care about fluff, the petty stuff in the daily grind.

Instead, we desire, we long to be at Your throne or better yet,
in Your lap and wrapped in Your loving arms of grace.

So I must come and linger;
but first, I must kneel at the Cross of Calvary one more time . . .
to remind me of Jesus' awesome gift of forgiveness.
And then on to His tomb where He broke free so that we also
can choose to break free.
I am so grateful for it all—
the work of all three of You: Father, Son . . .
and without the Holy Spirit's continuous comfort and quiet
words in my spirit every moment, where would I be?
Thank You, God.

*"So whenever we are in need, we should come bravely before the throne
of our merciful God.
There we will be treated with undeserved kindness,
and we will find help."
Hebrews 4:16, CEV*

My Bleeding Heart

*"But Mary treasured up all these things and
pondered them in her heart."*
Luke 2:19, NIV

"And a sword will pierce through your own soul also . . ."
Luke 2:35, AMP

Time has passed, and the gushing, throbbing flow
has finally slowed to a trickle, but my wounded heart
still seeps a little . . . every day.
Our hearts are wounded, pierced clear through by the shocking,
senseless death of suicide.
Parents never plan to bury one of their children and certainly not
by a death of their own choosing . . . and it is
still gut-wrenchingly hard to put feelings into words.

But we don't suffer alone.
We have friends, yes, but they don't live inside us.
They don't know the ache that
clings to our hearts every moment.
But there is Someone who does know and His name is Jesus.

I am comforted to read that He hurts when His children hurt.
He cries when we cry . . . and
"when they bleed, He bleeds; when they die, He dies."
Psalm 72:14, MSG.

There is another Psalm that says "the Lord cares deeply
when His loved ones die."
Psalm 116:15, NLT

I think that I can understand a bit of Jesus' mother's pain,
for I too, am a mother who has a pierced heart . . .
but not for long.

Her Son and our Savior died for us and now He lives!
He sits at the right hand of God in heaven . . . but not for long.

Soon heaven will empty as everyone zooms toward planet Earth.
Now is the moment they and we have been waiting for.
The Heavenly Hosts are going to free our children
from the bondage of Earth.

In the twinkle of an eye, our hearts will be mended when we
are all reunited with our resurrected loved ones.
And His Love and blood makes it all possible.
Thank You, Jesus!

May I Have Your Heart?

"So, what do you think?
With God on our side like this, how can we lose?
If God didn't hesitate to put everything on the line for us, embracing our
condition and exposing Himself to the worst by sending His own Son,
is there anything else
He wouldn't gladly and freely do for us?
And who would dare tangle with God
by messing with one of God's chosen?
Who would dare even to point a finger?
The One who died for us—who was raised to life for us—
is in the presence of God at this very moment sticking up for us.
Do you think anyone is going to be able to drive a wedge
between us and Christ's love for us?"
Romans 8:31–37, MSG

Precious Lord,
Is there anything You couldn't or wouldn't do for us?
You forgive our sins—every one.
You heal our diseases—every one.
You redeemed us from a fiery reward—saving our lives.
You crown us with love and mercy—a paradise crown!
You wrap us in goodness and eternal beauty.

You renew our youth—we are always young in Your presence . . .
and all this bounty is but a tip of the "eternal iceberg."
Psalm 103:2–4, MSG, paraphrased

To understand Your great Love, Lord, we are admonished
to focus on Calvary where You paid the ultimate price for sin
with Your own life.
And even while suffering not only the weight of our sin,
but the torturous cross,
Your thoughts were only about us:

"Printed over Him was a sign:
THIS IS THE KING OF THE JEWS,
one of the criminals hanging alongside cursed Him:

'Some Messiah You are! Save Yourself! Save us!'

But the other one made him shut up:

'Have you no fear of God? You're getting the same as Him.
We deserve this, but not Him—He did nothing to deserve this.'

Then he said,

'Jesus, remember me when You enter Your kingdom.'

He said,

'Don't worry, I will. You will join Me in paradise.'"
Luke 23:38–43, MSG

As sorrowful as Your suffering makes me, Jesus,
I am totally amazed
that You could think about someone else at such a time.
After all, just taking a breath was excruciating.
You had to push up against those spikes in Your feet
to take a gulp of air . . .

You Loved so much that You put aside Your pain
to answer the criminal—
who deserved what he got.
But he died knowing that he would rise to a new life
when You come in the clouds of glory.
How awesome You are, my Savior.

How can I not love You?
How can I not give You my heart, my all?

I plan to have all of eternity to thank You, love You, adore You,
and sing praises to Your Holy Name.

Confessions
of Suffering

Suffering is a Gift

*"There's far more to this life than trusting in Christ.
There's also suffering for Him.
And the suffering is as much a gift as the trusting."*
Philippians 1:29, MSG

Dear Lord,
Do we have to talk about suffering?
Trusting is hard too, but it is a much nicer word.

I'd hate to have to suffer like You did on Calvary,
but to follow You is to suffer . . .
there is no other way.

I used to worry about suffering for You, Lord,
but I no longer do.
Since the enemy took our son to the pit of death,
I now know suffering—intense, bitter suffering.

Then Jesus went to work on His disciples:

*"Anyone who intends to come with Me has to let Me lead.
You're not in the driver's seat; I Am.
Don't run from suffering; embrace it. Follow Me and I'll show you how.
Self-help is no help at all.*

*Self-sacrifice is the way, My way, to finding yourself, your true self.
What kind of deal is it to get everything you want but lose yourself?
What could you ever trade your soul for?"*
Matthew 16:24, MSG

Help me find my true self, Lord, my gift to You.
You drive; I'll ride along.
If there is more suffering; so be it . . .
as long as I have You with me.

Is Anyone Listening?

Where are You, God?
My mind says that You are in my heart,
but my heart is not so sure.
So much bad stuff happens with so little good stuff
to balance the scale.

I look up at the moon and stars in the clear, night sky and
wonder about the vastness of space.
Are You out there, God?

Sometimes I feel like a lonely child with her face
pressed against the glass.
She's not allowed to go outside, but the bustling activity going on
out there looks so inviting.

I am that little girl trapped inside the house, which feels like
it has become my prison.
I can only admire the outside world with my face
pressed against the glass.

Do you see that lonely, little girl, God?
When will she ever be free to explore, to love, to be herself?
Will she grow up trapped in a cycle of being
what everyone else expects her to be?
Or will she fly free?

The child in me cries out, and for what, she's not even sure.
She can't seem to give her inner words a voice.
Will You give them a voice, God?

It feels like I am always waiting, always wondering, always
hoping You are leading.
But You are so quiet, so like the dark, immensity of
space in which I am but a speck.

God, please teach my heart what my head understands—
and my heart will follow Your lead.
And by Your power,
I will fly free!

Is It Time Yet?

Father God,
How my heart aches for Your children
entangled in crashed cars or jet liners, in rapes, murders—
and that's just today's report.
It never ends!

How Your heart must ache for all the hurting people You have
created since the beginning of time.
It seems like we live in Sodom again.
Perhaps somewhere, a modern Noah is preaching
while building an ark.
Is it time yet?

It reminds me of the oft heard question from my children:
"Daddy, are we there yet?"
Children are always impatient and wiggly,
eager to be about the business of exploring new places.
They can barely wait for the motor to shut off before they escape
their confinement to play.

We tire of hearing the same old question, but they
never tire of asking it:
"Are we there yet?"

The adult version of that question has been on my mind since
a few years ago when suddenly and tragically
we were burying a child
long before his three score and ten years were up.

Now, the only question on my mind is:
Oh God, is it time to come home yet?
Is England's Big Ben about to bong out the midnight hour?
Is the steeple clock in Amsterdam ready to chime
for the last time?

I don't need to ask if You are ready—
You've been ready for thousands of years.
But . . . You are so patient, so unwilling for any of Your children
to miss out on eternity.

Yours, O Lord, is the greatness, the power, the glory,
the victory, and the majesty.
Everything in the heavens and on earth is Yours,
O Lord and we adore You as the One who is over all things.
And finally, it is time?
Yippee!

Get out of bed, children! Wake up!
Put your faces in the sunlight.
God's bright glory has risen for you.
The whole earth is no longer wrapped in darkness.
God is rising on us—
His sunrise glory breaks over us.
Look up! Look around!

Watch as they gather, watch as they approach you: our sons are
coming from great distances;
our tiny daughters are being carried by their nannies.

When we see them coming, we'll smile—big smiles!
Our hearts will swell and burst with happiness and joy!

He who has testified that He is coming, will come!
Please come soon, Lord Jesus.
1 Chronicles 29:11, NLT; Isaiah 60:1, MSG; Revelation 22:20, NIV, paraphrased

Rejecting Our Redeemer

"The servant grew up before God
—a scrawny seedling, a scrubby plant in a parched field.
There was nothing attractive about Him,
nothing to cause us to take a second look.
He was looked down on and passed over,
a man who suffered, who knew pain firsthand.

One look at Him and people turned away.
We looked down on Him, thought He was scum.
But the fact is, it was our pains He carried—

Our disfigurements, all the things wrong with us we thought
He brought it on Himself,
that God was punishing Him for His own failures.

But it was our sins that did that to Him, that ripped and tore
and crushed Him—our sins!

He took the punishment and made us whole.
Through His bruises we got healed.

We're all like sheep who've wandered off and gotten lost.
We've all done our own thing, gone our own way.
And God has piled all our sins, everything we've done wrong,
on Him, on Him."
Isaiah 53:2–6, MSG

Dear Lord,
I may think I have known rejection in my life, but when I read
about Your trauma in Isaiah, nothing in my life compares.

I am awed, humbled and amazed how You responded
to the children You created by going ahead
and dying to save us anyway.
Forgive me, Lord.

This Child Has Armor

There was once a tiny wisp of a child with golden curls,
bright eyes, and a captivating smile.

But this child, barely out of diapers, had already experienced
neglect, pain, and abandonment.
How could she ever survive in a grownup world that had all
those bad things—and more?
The answer can only come from the One who creates
special armor for children.

They may not yet know or understand
about the shield of faith or the sword of the Spirit,
But they have an innate, relentless search for love—
God's unconditional Love—with every beat
of their tiny hearts.

God has placed a longing for Himself, for eternity,
within every heart He has created, (Ecclesiastes 3:11, NIV),
and it' a longing that only He can fill.

God is huge, but He can fit inside the heart of a tiny child.
Nothing else will make a person of any size
feel whole though many
have tried other "pegs" of all shapes and sizes.
All have failed.
Only the eternity peg will fit.

And this fragile waif already knows and is searching for Him
who will fill up her tiny heart with His Love.
Already she loves Him who she has not yet met.

Time and years have tumbled after each other and an unthinkable
tragedy struck the family.
But through it all, she found Him faithful,
He whom her soul has craved.

He had been with her all along—from the bars in her crib,
through the pain of horrible loss.
He is Jesus Christ, her Knight and her Protective Armor.

Stuffing the Pain

*"In His kindness God called you to share in His eternal glory
by means of Christ Jesus.
So after you have suffered a little while, He will restore,
support, and strengthen you,
and He will place you on a firm foundation."*
1 Peter 5:10, NLT

I am way past childhood, Lord.
I am way past puberty and well into adulthood . . .
so why do I still do it?
Why can't I outgrow painful habits that started so long ago?

I was born a compliant child—fearful, doubtful, and silent . . .
except when my head was exploding with pain
and I had to cry out.

Sometimes the pain was so intense that all I could do was bang
my head in frustration on the bars of my crib.
Did I learn to stuff myself with food when I was very young?
Perhaps when I was barely out of diapers?

Of course, You saw me going back for second helpings then,
as You see me do it now.
Or the late night eating when no one is watching . . .
all are fast asleep.
It comforts me from the pain, for a few minutes anyway.

Perhaps it's not really about the food.

Perhaps I can relate just slightly to the troubled alcoholic who
wants to quit, but the body begs for just one more sip.

I want to eat to live and not the other way around, Lord.
I have often begged for You to seal my mouth shut with heavenly
duct tape or give me new taste buds that abhor donuts and
chocolate and ice cream and candy, and, and . . .

Perhaps I stuffed myself as a child instead of "telling it like it is."
That would have been wrong and I would have been
scolded for being mouthy.
I always knew my opinion did not matter . . .
no one ever heard it anyway.

Others had always spoken louder than me.
And I hated being the only one talking . . . and the only one who
was being stared at.

So silence ruled.
And silence led to invisibility
and invisibility has followed me all of my days.

Stuff the pain. Stuff the rage.
Stuff the sadness. Stuff the ignorance of others.
Stuff the cruelty of others.
Stuff it down, way down—all the feelings that bubble
up and beg to have a voice.

Eating is less harmful . . . to others, at least.
It only harms me, but not as bad as alcohol, right?
It only hurts me on the inside where I can't see
and puts pounds on the outside that I can unfortunately see . . .
and hate.
Lord, what is the answer here?
Is there one?
I hope so. I really do.

I desire to be released from the shackles of bad habits and the
lack of self-control and be set free.

I am relieved that You and I can talk so openly and
You never scold me, ever.
You Love me unconditionally and I love You for that.
Thanks, God.

*"In the day when I called, You answered me; and You strengthened me
with strength (might and inflexibility to temptation) in my inner self."*
Psalm 138:3, AMP

*"For here's what I'm going to do: . . . I'll give you a new heart, put a new spirit in
you. I'll remove the stone heart from your body and replace it with a heart
that's God-willed, not self-willed.*
*I'll put My Spirit in you and make it possible for you to do what I tell you
and live by My commands."*
Ezekiel 36:24, MSG

I Trump Rejection

My Dear Child,
I know you sometimes feel as though others are rejecting you,
so I am writing to gladden your heart.
*I absolutely delight in saving those who society rejects for whatever
reason; it does not matter in the least.*
I Love them no matter their shape, size, or past.

Let's talk about some of My friends from long ago.
Remember King David?
*He wasn't always a king, and he wasn't always
following after Me.*

There were times of terrible mistakes with heavy consequences.
Among other sins, he committed adultery and murder—back to back.
And he thought he was above the law and in the clear.
Wrong. Way wrong.
But he repented and sought after Me once more.

I remember him as the man after My own heart (1 Samuel 13:14, NIV)
even after all his sins!
Unbelievable, right?

And then there was Mary—My friend Mary Magdalene.
She was one of My faithful followers . . .
but she did not start out that way.
She had a sordid past.

I met her when she was flung at My feet,
accused of prostitution and worthy of stoning.
But I knew Mary's heart.

She longed for something different, something better than she had.
She longed to be saved from her life and together,
we did that.
Unbelievable, right?

No, very believable and miraculous.
I Am still in the miracle-working business, My Child.
Sometimes it may seem to you that I Am far away, but really,
I Am only a thought, a prayer away.

My Spirit lives within you when you choose Me.
So don't feel rejected.
I Love you and My opinion is the only one that counts.

Your Friend,
Jesus

Glory Follows Suffering

"Everything belongs to God, and all things were created by His power.
So God did the right thing when He made Jesus perfect by suffering,
As Jesus led many of God's children to be saved
and to share in His glory".
Hebrews 2:10, CEV

"And since we are His children, we are His heirs.
In fact, together with Christ we are heirs of God's glory.
But if we are to share His glory, we must also share His suffering."
Romans 8:17, NLT

Dear Lord,
I have read these texts before, but I gave them little thought . . .
because, quite honestly, I did not want to think about them.
I did not want to think about suffering, and more specifically,
painful persecution in any form.

I was at such a low place after my son's death that I started
searching the Bible for specific texts that would help
the ache in my heart.
I came across these . . .and noted excitedly, there is glory, but
first, there must be suffering—sharing in Your suffering.

We now understand suffering, even persecution,
for we are living it!
We were shot out of a canon and straight into the darkness
of hell when our son died suddenly and tragically.

After months had passed and we were surprisingly still alive, I
could finally hear You speaking to my heart about suffering:

My Dear Child,
Suffering is difficult to comprehend until one is forced
to live it.
Now you have a taste of what I suffered on Calvary to set you free.

135

First, the suffering, and then comes the glory . . . all a part
of the plan to save My children, once and for all.
Suffering must come.
Gold must be refined before it is useful.
Suffering leads to complete submission and refines your
character in preparation for eternity.
So don't waver.
Keep searching My Words.
In them, you will be continually reminded that you can cast
all your anxieties on Me because
I care for you.
1 Peter 5:7, NIV, paraphrased

Love,
Jesus

"Friends, when life gets really difficult, don't jump to the conclusion
that God isn't on the job.
Instead, be glad that you are in the very thick of what Christ experienced.
This is a spiritual refining process, with glory
just around the corner."
1 Peter 4:12–13, MSG

When Words Fail

Dear Friend,
Our hearts blend with yours in your pain.
You have suffered the loss of someone you dearly loved.
Words fail at a time like this; there just aren't any.

Instead, there are plenty of "if onlys" and "whys" . . . just ask us.
We could fill a page, hand it to you, and you'd fill another.
Those of us who grieve have understanding hearts
. . . and we feel your pain.

All we can say at these awful moments is "we are so sorry,"
hug you tightly,
and then point you to the risen Christ.
For it is in Him that we put our faith and trust.
He alone knows your pain.
He alone will hold you tightly in His embrace.
He alone will make it right—when He comes again.

"Your sun will never set or your moon go down.
I, the LORD, will be Your everlasting light, and your days of sorrow
will come to an end."
Isaiah 60:20, CEV

". . . I will turn their mourning into gladness;
I will give them comfort and joy instead of sorrow."
Jeremiah 31:12, NIV

Hope of Heaven

". . . and we rejoice in the hope of the glory of God.
Not only so, but we also rejoice in our sufferings, because we know
that suffering produces perseverance; perseverance, character;
and character, hope.
And hope does not disappoint us, because God has poured out His love
into our hearts by the Holy Spirit, whom He has given us."
Romans 5:2–5, NIV

Dear God,
Thank You for these encouraging words.
I know that I can trust You to produce this hope in me.
But the process of getting there is not easy . . .
the first word is "suffering"
and none of us want this, but it doesn't sound
like we can bypass any of the steps.

We have come face to face with the enemy as we,
with tear-stained faces, were forced to look down upon our
beloved son, asleep in death.

How I would love to have been able to shake his shoulder gently
or whisper in his ear and wake him up.
But the enemy of death is in charge at this moment in time,
but not for long!

Your Son Jesus will come as He has promised and He will shout
victory's refrain and our son, like so many others,
will come up out of his dusty grave!

The enemy of death will take no more prisoners.
Our suffering will be behind us forever.
Home at last!

Cradled in His Hand

Be merciful to me, O Lord, for I am in distress; my eyes grow
weak with sorrow, my soul and my body with grief.
My times are in Your hands; deliver me from my enemies
and from those who pursue me.

But I trust in You, O Lord; I say, "You are my God."
How great is Your goodness and in the shelter of Your presence You hide me.
Let Your face shine on me and save me in Your unfailing Love.
Psalm 31:9-20, NIV, paraphrased

Heavenly Father,
You are teaching me that trusting is everything, but life is hard.
The enemy is always lurking nearby to rush
at me in a moment of weakness and sabotage our relationship.

Please keep me filled with the rich current of Your Love,
for You are the only Power Source
that will make a permanent difference in my life.

I trust You to continue holding me in the palm of Your hand
and up close to Your heart where I fall asleep,
warm and content.

*"If You wake me each morning with the sound of Your loving voice, I'll go to
sleep each night trusting in You.
Point out the road I must travel; I'm all ears, all eyes before You.
Save me from my enemies, God—You're my only hope!
Teach me how to live to please You, because You're my God.
Lead me by Your blessed Spirit
into cleared and level pastureland."*
Psalm 143:8–10, MSG

In the precious Name of Jesus,
Thank You. Amen.

Preparation
for Heaven

Bring Up a Child

*"Direct your children onto the right path, and when they are older,
they will not leave it."*
Proverbs 22:6, NLT

Lord, thank You for this promise.
I lift up my children daily to You, for only You can protect them,
guide them, knock on the door of their hearts,
and entreat them
to let You enter their lives and be their Friend.

I must admit that I have pangs of guilt amidst the stabs of pain.
For one of my children was started on the path,
but he chose to snuff out his light himself . . .
so how does this text apply to him?

My question remains suspended in the air between us.
I suspect no answer will come . . .
this side of heaven.
I also suspect this is where trust comes in, right Lord?

I choose to trust that You will keep each promise in Your Word,
and all of them joined together, end to end,
include all of Your precious children.
For You are in the business of saving lives, not destroying them.

So keep knocking on the door of our hearts.
Keep directing our paths.
Eternity is where Your eyes are focused . . . and so are mine.

Keep On Trusting Me

My Dear Child,
I know the road of life seems endlessly painful, but keep trusting in Me.
Even though the death of your precious son makes you want to doubt, don't.
Keep trusting that I have everything under control.
It's easier to believe in what you see,
rather than what My Word says, but human sight is flawed.
My Word is not.
Others may tell you their personal truth, but they could be wrong
unless they were with Me when I laid
the earth's foundation (Job 38:4, NIV).
I created you. I will never fail you.
My One and Only Son died to save you.
And I have a mansion prepared for you . . . up here, where I AM.

My Words are Truth so take them to heart:

"As for God, His way is perfect; the word of the Lord is tried.
He is a Shield to all those who trust and take refuge in Him."
2 Samuel 22:31, AMP

"My people, you are My witnesses and My chosen servant.
I want you to know Me, to trust Me, and understand that I alone am God.
I have always been God; there can be no others."
Isaiah 43:10, CEV

". . . you trust God, don't you? Trust Me.
There is plenty of room for you in My Father's home.
If that weren't so, would I have told you that I'm on My way to get a room
ready for you? And if I'm on My way to get your room ready,
I'll come back and get you so you can live where I live."
John 14:1–3, MSG

I can be trusted.

All My Love, Jesus

Enemy Bully

"You saved me from the bullies.
That's why I'm thanking You, God, all over the world.
That's why I'm singing songs that rhyme Your Name."
2 Samuel 22:46–48, MSG

"What did he ever do to you?" we explode in anger.
"Why don't you pick
on somebody your own size?"
These questions are very familiar . . .I have heard them since
my childhood, and I probably
repeated them a time or two to my own children as well.

Nobody likes a bully.
Nobody likes to see big kids pick on little kids who are too weak
to defend themselves against a big bully.

Those of us who witness such an encounter will likely
defend the weaker one while
telling the bully to pick on someone his own size . . .
or better yet,
don't pick on anyone at all.

I'd like to tell Satan to pick on someone else . . .
but I'd rather he pick on no one.
He's a bully, an evil bully.

He bullied our son . . . and we were not there to defend him.
But I cannot live in the valley of regrets . . .
I must go on, wrapped in the Love of Jesus,
knowing that He always comes to the aid of His kids . . .
including mine.

Dear Jesus,
You are the only One who is strong enough to take on our bully
enemy, Satan, and his evil angels.

Fight him for me today and every day and keep fighting
him until You come and take care of him for good.

Thank You for Your promise that trouble will not rise up
a second time (Nahum 1:9, NIV).
Heaven without Satan . . . what a blessing!
I can hardly wait for eternity to begin!

New Clothes

*"This image of planting a dead seed and raising a live plant
is a mere sketch at best,
but perhaps it will help in approaching the mystery of the resurrection body—
but only if you keep in mind that when we're raised,
we're raised for good, alive forever!*

*The corpse that's planted is no beauty,
but when it's raised, it's glorious.
Put in the ground weak, it comes up powerful.*

*The seed sown is natural; the seed grown is supernatural—
same seed, same body,
but what a difference from when it goes down
in physical mortality
to when it is raised up in spiritual immortality!"*
1 Corinthians 15:42–44, MSG

Dear Lord,
How I long for the new life You have promised
as my days on this earth lengthen.
How I long for the sparkling "new clothes" we will exchange
our old, tattered ones for as soon
as the trumpet sounds!
Meanwhile, we face more sad good-byes, but each one
brings us closer to Your coming!
Come Lord Jesus,
Amen.

First, Feed Them

Dear Lord,
I hunger and thirst for Your righteousness and
I'm certainly not the only one, am I?
You have many children, just like me, who are starving for Truth.
How can You reach all of us?

If I go by Your example,
You often started with yummy, tummy food . . .
and then when people were nourished and comfortable,
You fed them from Your abundance of spiritual food.

I shall do likewise, for I choose to follow
in Your footsteps, for You have said,

*"Never walk away from someone who deserves help;
your hand is God's hand for that person."*
Proverbs 3:27, MSG

Lord, You know my neighbor.
She is weak, fearful, and destitute of earthly goods.
She has always avoided me . . . if I opened my mouth.
Thank You for impressing me not to "preach,"
but to buy her groceries.
We have done so, plus I have shared fresh vegetables, soup,
casseroles, and fresh bread, warm from the oven.

It is amazing, Lord.
Now my neighbor is not only thankful for the food,
she is hungry for You . . . but she doesn't quite realize it yet.
She has hesitantly started asking questions—wondering who I am
and more importantly, who You are!

Thank You for leading us so gently.
Thank You for opening the door wide enough to let everyone in . . .
just as we are.

Thank You for the blessing of abundant food for our
nourishment and pleasure.

Thank You for teaching us that the way to reach the heart is truly
through the tummy.

Thank You for Your wonderful example . . . first to feed them
and then to share the Bread of Life.

Love,
Your Daughter

*"Jesus called His disciples together and told them,
'I feel sorry for these people.
They have been with Me for three days, and they don't have anything to eat.
I don't want to send them away hungry. They might faint on their way home.'"*
Matthew 15:32, CEV

*"He will answer them,
'I'm telling the solemn truth: Whenever you failed to do
one of these things to someone who was being overlooked or ignored,
that was Me—you failed to do it to Me.'"*
Matthew 25:45, MSG

Only Bricks and Mortar

Dear Lord,
I am glad You know all things.
For sure, You are the only One who knows when You
are coming back again.

I grew up with, "get ready, be ready"
from mother's lips to my ears
and still You have not come.
Obviously, we aren't ready yet.

Not only are homes and families breaking up, but so are churches.
More families are leaving the church, Lord.
They leave for all kinds of reasons . . .
even if the order and content of the service is not to their liking.
What is that about?

Does our conduct please You?
What about our different tastes in music or preaching style?
Are You in those decisions?
What would You like in Your service, Lord?

I want to praise You anywhere, anytime, and I don't have to be
inside a building with a steeple on top, do I?

A building is just bricks and mortar.
Perhaps You don't even get an invitation into all churches
and if that is true, how shameful!
What a blessing we miss out on.

Lord, I want to be where You are.
I want to live to serve You, no matter where or when.
I want to be in heaven with You, no matter the cost.
For You are the One I praise.

*"Here's what I want: Give me a God-listening heart
so I can lead Your people well,
discerning the difference between good and evil.
For who on their own is capable of leading Your glorious people?"*
1 Kings 3:9, MSG

*"You also must obey the Lord—you must worship Him
with all your heart and remember the great things
He has done for you."*
1 Samuel 12:24, CEV

*"May the words of my mouth and the meditation of my heart
be pleasing in Your sight, O Lord, my Rock and my Redeemer."*
Psalm 19:14, NIV

Ignoring the Enemy

He walks, but he leaves no footprints.
He talks, but the sounds are internal and we fool ourselves
into thinking it is our own thoughts we hear.

What kind of enemy is this?
It is the enemy of our souls and we ignore him
as if he does not exist.
Big mistake! Huge!

We are used to an enemy who leaves footprints and we can see
where to attack.
We have grown up on wars, either suffered first hand or
read about in history books.

So who is this enemy that we can't see . . . or hear?
He is the roaring lion, (1 Peter 5:8, NIV).
He is the robber and murderer, (John 10:10, NIV).
He is the father of lies, (John 8:44, NIV) and he holds
the power of death (Hebrews 2:14, NIV).

He is invisible to our eyes . . .
but he is a fearsome warrior nonetheless.
His army is millions strong . . . and also invisible.
And his plan is to bring us to his side, so he won't die alone.

Are we prepared to fight an invisible foe?
How do we arm ourselves against something we cannot see?

Our fight it not against flesh and blood but against the spiritual
forces of evil in the heavenly realms.
Ephesians 6:12, NIV, paraphrased

"And that about wraps it up.
God is strong, and He wants you strong.

*So take everything the Master has set out for you,
well-made weapons of the best materials and put them to use
so you will be able to stand up to everything
the devil throws your way.*

*This is no afternoon athletic contest that we'll walk away from
and forget about in a couple of hours.
This is for keeps, a life-or-death fight to the finish against the
devil and all his angels."*
Ephesians 6:10–12, MSG

My Words

"A word aptly spoken is like apples of gold in settings of silver."
Proverbs 25:11, NIV

"They enjoyed the sweet taste of wickedness, letting it melt under their tongue."
Job 20:12, NLT

Dear Lord,
Words surely carry muscle, don't they?
By the verses state above, they can either be sweet or bitter,
falling at opposite ends of the spectrum.

Kind words can bring healing, encourage the lonely,
change the course of a life,
or push someone through to the finish line.
Words are powerful—power for good or power for evil.

Words can also discourage or bring sadness
to someone's countenance.
Words can hurt and even bring on an untimely death.
We can apologize for them, but we can never reel them back in—
they are left to float in the air forever and
often remembered . . . even longer.

151

Perhaps this is the reason there are so many texts of scripture that caution us to be careful about our words and the power of this small but mighty group of muscles.

Lord, let my words be an instrument of Your peace.
I cannot say it better than You have in Your Word,
so I will let it speak for itself.

"With the tongue we praise our Lord and Father, and with it we curse men, who have been made in God's likeness."
James 3:9, NIV

"Likewise the tongue is a small part of the body, but it makes great boasts. Consider what a great forest is set on fire by a small spark."
James 3:5, NIV

"Post this at all the intersections, dear friends: Lead with your ears, follow up with your tongue, and let anger straggle along in the rear. God's righteousness doesn't grow from human anger."
James 1:19–20, MSG

59 Minutes of Fellowship

Dear God,
We have come before You today to worship You in praise
and thanksgiving for Your many blessings.

We hope You are pleased that we are rearranging the order
of service to bring more glory and honor to You.

Our choice of music pleases us and we hope
that it pleases You . . . but our style does not suit everyone and
some have chosen to leave and worship elsewhere.

You will notice that the atmosphere
is charged with excitement.
We like to keep things moving at a quick pace so that we
can get to dinner on time.

Nothing is quite so satisfying as a quick sample of
Christ's body followed by a multi-course meal of our favorite
foods to pig out on . . .

So, God, sit back, relax and enjoy our full fifty-nine
minutes of fellowship.

*"Who has known the mind of the Lord or been able
to give Him advice?"*
Isaiah 40:13, NCV

59 Minutes Is Never Enough

Heavenly Father,
I must linger in Your Presence today where I feel Your soft
breath upon my cheek and Your sweet Spirit quickens my heart.
The lights have been turned off
and I hear the faint clicking of keys . . .
the deacon is waiting to lock the doors . . .
but I am reluctant to leave just yet.
The world is so cold, so calloused.
I want to stay and experience the fullness of Your love, joy, peace
to equip me for survival in the day-to-day struggle.
Satan and all his evil angels wish to sift me like wheat, but I
know You are all powerful and he is not
and under Your wings I shall stay.

Luke 22:31, NIV; Psalm 61:4, CEV, paraphrased

Asleep on Duty

Lord, please wake us up!
We have been on night watch so long while waiting for Your coming
that we have fallen into a deep slumber.

The enemy never sleeps and he's armed and dangerous!
He is as active as ever—stealthily driving his troops deeper and deeper
into the ranks of our homes, schools, churches, and hearts:
driving wedges between viewpoints,
severing parent from parent, and children from parents
and tossing his wrecking ball at our every dream and emotion.

His aim is accurate and he knows exactly what will keep us
occupied with ourselves . . . and no longer desperately looking
and longing for You to come.

What is left but to "steal and kill and destroy" (John 10:10, NIV)
from hearts that aren't totally surrendered to You?

You said for us to occupy until You come
but You had spiritual quests in mind, didn't You?
You seek tirelessly to save every thoughtless child
for You do not want any of Your died-for children
to miss out on eternity.

Lord, use me in any way You desire to reach out to Your children.
I give You permission to speak through me.
Allow me to be an empty vessel that You can fill to overflowing
with Your Love and grace so that others may see Your
reflection on my face.

And let it be all to Your glory for eternity's sake.

*"We also know that the Son of God has come and has given us
understanding so that we can know the True One.
And our lives are in the True One and in His Son, Jesus Christ.
He is the true God and the eternal life."*
I John 5:20, NCV

Love One Another

*"Your beauty and love chase after me every day of my life.
I'm back home in the house of God
for the rest of my life."*
Psalm 23:6, MSG

*Dear Children,
"I've Loved you the way My Father has Loved Me.
Make yourselves at home in My Love.
If you keep My commands, you'll remain intimately
at home in My Love.
That's what I've done—kept My Father's commands and
made Myself at home in His Love."*

*Hold fast to the Truth I have shared with you,
but don't hold on so tightly that you forget to
let Me shine through you.*

*It's good to huddle, but be genuine.
Look out for the lonely, famished, neglected ones . . .
they are starved for Me, so share My Love with them.*

*I know you are broken and hurting too . . . I have not forgotten.
But when you realize that I can fill you up so full
that you are bursting at the seams, it's okay to "leak" a bit,
for when you do, others will receive your
shared blessings and come to know that I Love them too.*

155

*"I've told you these things for a purpose: that My joy might be
your joy, and your joy wholly mature.
This is My command: Love one another the way I Loved you.
This is the very best way to Love.
Put your life on the line for your friends.*

You are My friends when you do the things I command you . . ."

*". . . if God Loved us like this, we certainly ought to Love each other.
No one has seen God, ever.
But if we Love one another, God dwells deeply within us,
and His Love becomes complete in us—perfect Love!"*
John 15:9–14; 1 John 4:11–12, MSG

*Love Always,
Jesus*

Last Enemy Down!

*". . . Death initially came by a man, and resurrection from death came by a man.
Everybody dies in Adam; everybody comes alive in Christ.*

*But we have to wait our turn:
Christ is first, then those with Him at His Coming, the grand
consummation when, after crushing the opposition, He hands over
His kingdom to God the Father.*

*He won't let up until the last enemy is down -
and the very last enemy is death!"*
1 Corinthians 15:21–26, MSG

This verse is a precious promise of God's faithfulness.
Death is our worst enemy.
It always has been and it always will be until Jesus comes again.

Satan has been a lion, roaring his rage since
he was cast out of heaven.
One after another, his attempts to destroy Jesus failed and his
roar has become deafening in our ears.

But thankfully, Satan has no power
over the Prince of Heavenly Power!
Total and complete victory belongs to Jesus, and because He
lives, we also have victory over sin and death!

Yes, the enemy completely failed, but he still roams the earth,
seeking whom he may devour (1 Peter 5:8, NIV).
Satan has been allowed to manage this earth for a while but
humanely. God is about to post a "No Trespassing" sign
on planet Earth and set a demolition date.
Sin and death will be no more!

This promise is personal and creates great longing in me.
I lost my son.
The author of death snatched him in the prime of his young
adulthood, and buried him in the dark earth.
I can almost hear him chuckling himself . . .

"Where I go, you go. You are one of many.
When I die, I am not dying alone. I'll see to that."

So he roams the earth, searching for the weak, the helpless, the
hopeless, the threatened, the imprisoned,
the lonely and depressed.

"These are worthless," he rages.
"Who will miss them?
I'll take them down to destruction the most hurtful way I can . . .
I'll get them to kill themselves; to break one of my Enemy's
precious rules. That will guarantee they are mine! All mine!"

But Satan misunderstands the heart of God and His Son,
Jesus Christ, our Savior.
It is His tears, His blood, that paid for us so long ago.
He wants to bring us all to heaven with Him,
not lock us out.

Death may seize us in a grip of grief and fear . . . for awhile, but
graves will burst open when Jesus shouts from the skies.

No enemy can keep our loved ones in the ground.
They will spring forth in newness of life,
joyously celebrating their King.

*"If we get included in Christ's sin-conquering death, we also get included
in His life-saving resurrection.
We know that when Jesus was raised from the dead it was a signal
of the end of death-as-the-end.
Never again will death have the last word."*
Romans 6:8–10, MSG

Come soon Jesus. I love You!

Fresh Fruits from God's Orchard

Running on Empty?

In the night hours, God spoke to my heart.

*My Child,
In your day-to-day busy lifestyle, is your "temple tank" running
on empty or full?*

The following day, that question returned to my mind.
What exactly did He mean?
Then I remembered He had mentioned "the Fruits of the Spirit"
as a good place to begin studying for the answer.

Love

Heavenly Father,
You have a Love for us that never fails.
Your Word is chock full of the word, "love" and the longing You
have for us to love You in return.

Please fill me with Your perfect Love and live
forever in my heart.
Amen.

Joy

"But let all those who take refuge and put their trust in You rejoice;
let them ever sing and shout for joy,
because You make a covering over them and defend them;
let those also who live Your Name be joyful
in You and be in high spirits."
Psalm 5:11, AMP

Dear Lord,

You also wrote through the psalmist that . . .
"weeping may endure for a night, but joy comes in the morning."
Psalm 30:5, AMP

Sorrow takes so much energy, Lord, that it feels like
I will never have joy again.
Perhaps a little of Your "high-octane additive" will help.
Please add enough super-charged joy to my tank today to
jump start my life again.
And even when problems arise like dark clouds;
low and threatening,
help me to look for joy in spite of the dumpster-diving,
roller coaster emotions that swirl around me.
I am grateful that You reign . . .
and I will hold You to Your promise that joy will
come again, in the morning.
Amen.

Peace

*Because we have sought the Lord our God,
yearning for Him with all our desire,
He has given us rest and peace on every side.
And even when we lie down to sleep, You alone, O Lord,
will keep us safe.*
2 Chronicles 14:7; Psalm 4:8, NIV, paraphrased

*"When people are saying, all is well and secure,
and there is peace and safety,
then in a moment unforeseen destruction (ruin and death)will come upon them
as suddenly as labor pains come upon a woman
with child; and they shall by no means escape,
for there will be no escape."*
1 Thessalonians 5:3, AMP

Dear Lord,
These texts are at opposing ends of the spectrum.
Do we need a reality check?
You promise peace, but there is no peace in this world today . . .
far from it.

Yes, we hear peace phrases spoken by both preachers and politicians,
but according to the last text, there is no peace.
So if there is no peace, how do we get this fruit?

*My Child,
The only peace you will ever have is in Me.
This world does not offer peace—though it promises you many things.
Some things are good, but most lead your mind far away
from Truth, and from Me.
Please lean on Me.
You will never be too heavy for Me to hold.
I have much to teach you; to share with you so you will
be strengthened for troublesome times ahead.
Yes, many will cry "peace and safety" from now until I return,
but don't be misled.*

I alone Am the Way, the Truth, and the Life.
And it is in these three that you will find the
fruit of perfect peace.

"You will keep in perfect peace him whose mind is steadfast,
because he trusts in You."
Isaiah 26:3, NIV

Patience

"There's more to come: We continue to shout our praise
even when we're hemmed in with troubles, because we
know how troubles can develop passionate patience in us,
and how that patience in turn forges the tempered steel of virtue,
keeping us alert for whatever God will do next.

In alert expectancy such as this, we're never left feeling shortchanged.
Quite the contrary—we can't round up enough containers to hold
everything God generously pours into our lives
through the Holy Spirit!"
Romans 5:3–5, MSG

"May God, who gives this patience and encouragement,
help you live in complete harmony with each other,
as is fitting for followers of Christ Jesus."
Romans 15:5, NLT

This is a tall order, Lord,
trying to live in harmony with all the other "bratty"
human beings You created.

It seems like conflict or avoiding conflict is a part of our daily routine:
bosses can't get along with employees and employees
can't get along with each other.

Husbands and wives are in strife day in and day out.
And then there are the children.
We love them, Lord, but they are the only "home appliance"
that doesn't come with an instruction manual!

There isn't a day that goes by that we don't have conflict with our
toddlers and teens and all ages in between!

Father, please give me a prescription for patience
with plenty of refills.
And if it is one of the juicy fruits of the Spirit, then I need to
be swimming in fruit cocktail!

I know I can count on You to help me with all Your
created beings, great or small.
Thank You, Amen.

Kindness

*"The Word became a human being and lived here with us.
We saw His true glory, the glory of the only Son of the Father.
From Him all the kindness and all the truth
of God have come down to us."*
John 1:14, CEV

*"He who earnestly seeks after and craves righteousness,
mercy, and loving-kindness will find life in addition to righteousness
(uprightness and right standing with God) and honor."*
Proverbs 21:21, AMP

*"But You, O Lord, are a God merciful and gracious,
slow to anger and abounding in mercy and loving-kindness and truth."*
Psalm 86:15, AMP

*"The Lord is always kind to those who worship Him, and He
keeps His promises to their descendents."*
Psalm 103:17, CEV

Heavenly Father,
Your Word is so full of texts about Your kindness that I had a
hard time narrowing it down to just a few.

You give so much overwhelming evidence
that I am blown away by my often less-than-kind words
to You and to others.

Please empower me to treat Your children with the same
kindness You willingly shower on me.
I want to be just like You when I "grow up."
I want to clop along in a pair of Your huge shoes, following the
giant footprints You leave for me.

I won't fall down because You hold my small hand firmly in Your
big one; guiding me in Your unfailing Love.
Because You are so rich in grace and kindness,
You have purchased my freedom with the blood of Your Son Jesus,
Who forgives our sins.
What more could I ask for?

*So when I need my temple tank re-filled, I will bravely come
before the throne of my merciful God
and there I will be treated with kindness I do not deserve
and the help You so willingly and graciously give.*
Hebrews 4:16, NLT, paraphrased

Goodness

"And [God] Who provides seed for the sower and bread for eating will also provide and multiply your [resources for] sowing and increase the fruits of your righteousness {which manifests itself in active goodness, kindness, and charity}."
2 Corinthians 9:10, AMP

"He did this that He might clearly demonstrate through the ages to come the immeasurable (limitless, surpassing) riches of His free grace (His unmerited favor) in his [His] kindness and goodness of heart toward us in Christ Jesus."
Ephesians 2:7, AMP

Dear Lord,
I don't tell you often enough how good You are to me.
You are my Sun and Shield.
You give me grace and glory.
You, gracious Lord, do not withhold any good thing!

We live in a land of plenty and for that, I am so grateful.
Help me to willingly share Your goodness with those around me, both near and far.
Psalm 84:11, NLT, paraphrased

Faithfulness

"God's love is meteoric, His loyalty astronomic, His purpose titanic, His verdicts oceanic.
Yet in His largeness nothing gets lost; not a man, not a mouse, slips through the cracks."
Psalm 36:5–6, MSG

Merciful and Loving Father,
Your kindness and faithfulness extends to the skies,
which means there is no limit to Your care and example for us.
Psalm 36:5, AMP, paraphrased

Thankfully, I am protected on all sides.
You will save me from the slanders and reproaches of those
who are evil and would just as soon trample me
underfoot or in other ways cause me pain.
Relief is a mere breath away . . . a prayer is all that's needed.
You are always waiting, listening for the throb of my heart
as it beats in time with Yours.
May I recognize Your Truth, mercy and faithfulness every day
and seek to respond in kind to others
whom You have called me to serve.
Thank You, Amen.
Psalm 57:3, NIV, paraphrased

Gentleness

HE—

hushes the storm to a calm, gentle whisper.
Psalm 107:29, AMP

has a gentle Spirit that leads us in the right path.
Psalm 143:10, CEV

tells us that a gentle answer deflects anger.
Proverbs 15:1, NLT

tells us that gentle speech breaks down rigid defenses.
Proverbs 25:15, MSG

encourages us to take His yoke and learn from Him for He is gentle.
Matthew 11:29, NIV

asks us to choose internal beauty that will not fade; a gentle, quiet spirit.
1 Peter 3:4, NIV

*asks us to be humble, kind, meek and patiently put up with each other
and finally, love each other as God's chosen people.*
Ephesians 4:2; Colossians 3:12 paraphrased

Dear God,

I understand from Colossians 3:12–14, NIV, that you want me to
dress in the wardrobe You have picked out for me:

I am to be compassionate, kind, humble, have quiet strength,
disciplined, be even-tempered, content with second place,
and quick to forgive an offense.
In fact, I am to forgive as quickly and as completely
as You forgive me.

Whew! That's quite a laundry list, but You are not finished
dressing me. On top of all the other garments
You want me to wear a coat of Love.
This is Your trademark garment; the one that has Your signature
on it—Your Designer label.

I looked closely and realized that this coat, which says
it's a one-size-fits-everyone number, looks rather simple
and undignified for my Magnificent God.
But then I study the label itself and notice that it is done in
"Signature Red."
I get it, Father.
This garment of Love fits me and everyone else who is interested
in "Heaven's Best" clothing line.
It is the only style You have created.

It is the only one needed.
And the label has been written with a pen
dipped in the precious blood of Jesus
and written with His gentle hand.

I no longer need to shop.
I have found the coat that fits me best.
I choose to wear it and be just like its Designer.
He has time-tested the attributes He encourages me to live
and by Your grace and with Your power, I will.

I Love You.

". . . And regardless of what else you put on, wear love.
It's your basic, all-purpose garment.
Never be without it."
Colossians 3:14, MSG

Self-Control

The Law of the Lord is a lamp, and its teachings shine brightly.
Gentleness and self-control will lead you through life and there is no law against it.
Moderation is better than muscle, self-control better than political power. For
God has not given us a spirit of fear and timidity, but of power, love, and self-
discipline. So think clearly and exercise self-control.
Look forward to the gracious salvation that will come to you
when Jesus Christ is revealed to the world.
Proverbs 6:23, NIV; Proverbs 16:32, MSG; Galatians 5:23, NIV;
2 Timothy 1:7, NLT; 1 Peter 1:13, NLT, all paraphrased

Dear Lord,

You tell us that when we live Your way, You bring gifts into our lives,
much the same way that fruit appears in an orchard—
things like affection for others, exuberance about life, and serenity.

You help us develop a willing spirit to stick with things, a sense
of compassion in the heart, and a conviction that basic holiness
permeates things and people. Therefore, we find ourselves
involved in loyal commitments,
not needing to force our way in life and able to
marshal and direct our energies wisely.

Lord, You make it clear that legalism is helpless
in bringing this change about in us; it only gets in the way.
We used to treasure getting our own way and mindlessly
responding to what everyone else calls necessities, but no more.

These things are killed off for good—crucified.
Galatians 5:24, MSG, paraphrased

My temple has been running on fumes, Lord.
I choose to be emptied of myself in total surrender to You.
Please fill me plumb full—with all the luscious Fruits of the Spirit
and lead me in the way everlasting.

Thank You,
Amen

Rejoicing

Suffering in the Presence of Joy

Lord, I am hungry for joy; resilient, jubilant, bubbling joy.
Not the fairytale stuff, but the deep peace of abiding comfort
in spite of all the jilted dreams and tragedies of life.

I know You know what I mean,
even if I can't quite find the right words,
because Your Word is chock full of joy verses!
If I put them altogether and read them,
will I then have what I seek?
I'll give it a try.

"The revelation of God is whole and pulls our lives together.
The signposts of God are clear and point out the right road.
The life-maps of God are right, showing the way to joy.
The directions of God are plain and easy on the eyes.
God's reputation is twenty-four-carat gold, with a lifetime guarantee.
The decisions of God are accurate down to the nth degree."
Psalm 19:7, MSG

"You have turned my mourning into joyful dancing.
You have taken away my clothes of mourning
and clothed me with joy."
Psalm 30:11, NLT

But as for me, I will sing about Your power.
For You have been my refuge,
a place of safety when I am in distress.
Each morning I will sing with joy about Your unfailing
Love in the shadow of Your wings.
Psalm 59:16, 63:7, NLT, paraphrased

"The Lord is my strength and shield.
I trust Him with all my heart.
He helps me, and my heart is filled with joy.
I burst out in songs of thanksgiving."
Psalm 28:7, NLT

*"You will show me the way of life, granting me the joy
of Your presence and the pleasures of living with You forever."*
Psalm 16:11, NLT

*"Let us fix our eyes on Jesus, the author and perfecter of our faith,
who for the joy set before Him endured the cross,
scorning its shame,
and sat down at the right hand of the throne of God."*
Hebrews 12:2, NIV

Lord, I am stunned, taken aback, when I read
this last verse from Hebrews.
You endured the cross because of the joy set before You!
How can that be?

If You could feel joy in the midst of such agony and torture,
You will give me strength to feel joy
while I wait in eager anticipation
for the coming resurrection morning!

As it has been said before . . .

*"Weeping may last through the night,
but joy will come in the morning."*
Psalm 30:5, NLT

Yes! For sure on resurrection morning!
That's Your promise, Lord, and You keep Your promises.
Hallelujah!

Sunny Faces

Thank You, God, for the field of sunflowers this morning.
A sea of beautiful, golden yellow faces with a dark spot in the
middle as if they each had dunked their noses in creamy
chocolate and hadn't bothered
to lick it off, but then who would?

Each sunflower face was turned toward the sun . . . the huge fire ball
that their Creator told them would help them grow.
So they face it to get their daily growth and glow.

When the vast, colorful field faded from view,
You whispered in my ear,

"There is a lesson here, My Child. Don't miss it."

No, I don't want to miss the lesson.
Could it be that we need our faces turned upward too,
facing the Son of Righteousness
for our daily growth and glow?

*"And we, who with unveiled faces all reflect the Lord's glory,
are being transformed into His likeness with ever-increasing glory,
which comes from the Lord, who is the Spirit."*
2 Corinthians 3:18, NIV

Pipsqueak

What a cat!
Lord, You must have a great sense of humor.
A tiny, skinny, grey-tiger pipsqueak of a kitten "attacked" us as
we walked by a field of lush green.
He was all legs, fur, and purr in his insistence
that we take him home.

Poor little thing.
Who knew when he had last eaten? The least we could do
would be to give him a saucer of milk . . .
and hope he'd travel elsewhere.

After all, we already had one stray who ruled the roost and
no one wanted to mess with Samantha.
So we'd be foolish to introduce the two of them, wouldn't we?

But we went bonkers over this kitten.
He immediately showed us his tenacity, antics, and his
no-nonsense attempt to win us over—
and it worked.

He began to grow and put on weight and soon Pipsqueak became
"Pipy" for short and it fit his personality to a "T."

Within weeks we suffered a tragic loss.
One of our children died.
We fell into a deep pit of sorrow and never thought we'd climb
out into the sunshine ever again.

But all through our sorrow, Pipy delighted us with his game of
hide n' seek or tearing up the stairs lickety-split and
sliding around the corner on the tile floor as if
he was being chased by a ferocious jungle cat.

It has been several years now since Pipy found us
and we still can't stop laughing at him!

It wasn't long before we realized that God
had created Pipy just for us.
His timing was "purr-fect."
We needed a break from grief
and Pipy provides plenty of comic relief.

How great is our God!
Who would think He would care or bother
with a scrawny kitten!

He not only bothered, He made sure that Pipy
had plenty of personality
to help keep our hearts light with joy and laughter.

Thank You, God.
You think of everything—even the tiny details.
I just love You for that.

My Cup Overflows

*"Surely goodness and love will follow me all the days of my life,
and I will dwell in the house of the Lord forever."*
Psalm 23:6, NIV

Dear Lord,

This is absolute Truth for You cannot lie.
However, there have been days, even years,
when it hasn't "felt" true.
But You are showing me, inch by inch, feelings aren't reliable and
that You are the Only One I can rely on.

Hallowed be Your Name, precious Lord!
You mean everything to me.

*"So for the present you are also in sorrow (in distress and depressed);
but I will see you again and [then] your hearts will rejoice,
and no one can take from you your joy (gladness, delight)."*
John 16:22, AMP

Holy Spirit

You breathe fresh air into every Word of scripture.
You travel on the wings of God's Love, bringing His
Truth and grace into our darkened souls.
Thank You for turning the lights on and opening the windows,
which make the shadows scamper away and cause
us to fill our lungs with deep draughts
of Your joy-stuffed, fresh air.
Only You can answer our pleas with such swift, soft
understanding to our thirsting hearts.
Only You can satisfy our longing for God.
Thank You, Holy Spirit,
our invisible, comforting Friend.

Mud Pies

Dear God,

I may not be a good pie baker now, but when I was little,
I made the best mud pies.
They looked good enough to eat, but I knew they weren't
because they were just dirt and water.

The Bible says that we are just mud without Your breath and that
You care for us tenderly, knowing that we are
dust and easily broken.
You are amazingly gentle with us—like I had to be with
my mud pies or they would crack.

I just love these words about You, my Heavenly Parent:

"God is sheer mercy and grace; not easily angered,
He's rich in love.
He doesn't endlessly nag and scold, nor hold grudges forever.
He doesn't treat us as our sins deserve, nor pay us back in full for our wrongs.

For as the heavens are high above the earth, so great are His mercy and loving-
kindness toward those who reverently and worshipfully fear Him.
And as far as sunrise is from sunset, He has separated us from our sins.
As parents feel for their children, God feels for those who fear Him.
He knows us inside and out, keeps in mind that we're made of mud."
Psalm 103:8–14, MSG & AMP

"For you were made from dust, and to dust you will return."
Genesis 3:19, NLT

Mud pies are one thing, God,
but "dust to dust" is a hard concept for me.
How could I ever have known that I would go from baking mud
pies to visiting the cemetery where my boy is buried?

Again, I hold You to Your promise of restoration.
If all You needed to form Adam was a little mud and Your breath,
certainly You can make my son brand new.

Love always,
Your Daughter

Bouquets for Ashes

"Arise [from the depression and prostration in which circumstances
have kept you—rise to a new life]!
Shine (be radiant with the glory of the Lord), for your light has come,
and the glory of the Lord has risen upon you!"
Isaiah 60:1, AMP

"The sun shall no more be your light by day,
nor for brightness shall the moon give light to you . . . for the Lord shall be your
everlasting light, and the days of your mourning shall be ended."
Isaiah 60:19, 20, AMP

"The Spirit of God, the Master, is on me because God anointed me.
He sent me to preach good news to the poor, heal the heartbroken, announce
freedom to all captives,
pardon all prisoners.

God sent me to announce the year of His grace . . . to care for the needs of all
who mourn in Zion, to give them
bouquets of roses instead of ashes,
messages of joy instead of news of doom, a praising
heart instead of a languid spirit."
Isaiah 61:1, MSG

Dear Lord,

We are nearing the end of our journaling journey
into grief together.
You have pointed the way to Truth, hope, relief, trust
in ways a loving, heavenly Parent would do.

I can't say that my eyes will be dry or my sadness
completely disappear, but I know without a doubt
Who my Redeemer is, and it is You.

Thank You for reaching down into the ashes of my soul
and gently sifting about until You
uncovered a tiny rosebud—something that had escaped
the raging fire of tragedy that engulfed me.

The sweet, unblemished rose is Your sweet promise
that You will make all things new.
Hold me until You come and restore our family once again.

*"For as the earth bursts with spring wildflowers,
and as a garden cascades with blossoms, so the Master, God,
brings righteousness into full bloom . . ."*
Isaiah 61:1–3, 11, MSG

He's Mine!

*"But stop your crying and wipe away your tears.
Everything you have done for your children will not go unrewarded.
I will bring them back from death and from the land of the enemy."*
Jeremiah 31:16, Clear Word Bible (CWB)

My Dear Daughter,

*Do not weep over the death of your precious son.
He was a glowing ember in My heart long before he was a twinkle
in his daddy's eye . . . do you trust Me?
Trust in My power to restore him to you one day soon.
I have many other children who are also resting until I come.*

*Perhaps it will help you to hear a story
about another young son of Mine.
Some years ago, I had a precious son who loved the great outdoors.
He often hiked in the mountains or kayaked the rivers;
flying down the steep waterfalls into the foam below.*

*He was exhilarated and happy when he was celebrating My creation,
his face radiating sheer joy.
I had to throw back My head and laugh,
sharing in his excitement.
He had such gifts, but he had such sorrows too
and they got the best of him, with the enemy's help.*

This young man had gone camping and had parked in the cliffs
overlooking a canyon high in the Sierra Mountains.
He was missing for days and his mother was distraught with worry.
While a Search and Rescue team was dispatched to look for him,
I knew where he was, and I did not leave his side.

I gave a vision to a friend of his mother's and she awoke with a start.
The vision was in vivid color and she recognized the face of the young man
lying on a ledge, near the canyon floor by a stream.

Instantly awake, she was on her feet and sprinted to the phone.
With shaky fingers, she dialed the phone number of his mother
who hadn't been able to sleep;
her heart heavy with the devastating news that her son was dead.

My arms were wrapped tightly around her shoulders.
I had been sitting beside her for hours, holding her
and wiping the tears that streamed down her cheeks.

I ached to resurrect her son on the spot, but he, like your son,
will have to rest, until I come again.

The phone rang. It was his mother's friend, calling to check on her.
I helped her choke out the words,
"They found my son. He's dead."

Her friend responded, "I know," she said sadly.
"I saw him in a vision.
But you have to hear what else I saw.
He was not alone on that outcrop on the canyon wall,"
she began to chatter in breathless excitement.

"Jesus was standing on one side of your son and Satan on the other, and I
could hear them talking
just as clearly as if they were in my bedroom.
Jesus said calmly but firmly,

'Satan, you cannot have him any longer.
You have tormented him long enough and he's Mine.'

"To which Satan spat back, poking his bony finger toward Jesus,
'But he broke Your commandment: Thou shalt not kill.'"

"Jesus paused, allowing Satan's ringing words to exit the canyon.
Again He answered calmly but firmly,
'No, you don't understand, Satan.
He's Mine now . . . and forever!'"

My arm still around her shoulders, My daughter slowly hung up the phone
and we sat down together.
She began to relax in My embrace and I knew she understood.
She would one day soon have her precious gift I had given her back again.
She would embrace her son again.

See, My daughter, I have given special hearts to mothers to love their children
unconditionally for as long as they have them,
but they will continue to miss them all of their days
. . . until eternity.
But for My kids, it will seem like they had just closed their eyes in sleep when
I come to wake them up!
Continue to share your stories and the Good News, will you?

All My Love,
Jesus, Your Forever Friend

"For I will contend with him who contends with you,
and I will save your children."
Isaiah 49:25, NKJV

"I will turn their mourning into gladness and give them comfort and joy
instead of sorrow and pain."
Jeremiah 31:13, CWB

Go Tell

"Oh, thank God—He's so good! His love never runs out.
All of you set free by God, tell the world!"
Psalm 107:1–2, MSG

My Dear Daughter,
Thank you for allowing Me to accompany you on this
leg of your journey through grief.
How disappointed I would have been had you not invited Me!
Now go tell what you have learned; share your story with
hurting families everywhere.
Tell them of My great compassion, comfort, and undying Love.
Tell them My arms are long enough to encircle all of them.
Tell them My heart weeps along with theirs . . .
Tell them how you are finding what you were searching for . . . in Me.
Remember, the more you share your story,
the more you, yourself, will be comforted . . . it's a win/win.
So take Me with you wherever you go.
Go tell the rest of My hurting children that I Am coming soon
and only through Me, can their hearts be set free to enjoy eternity.
We are almost home for good.
Love, God

The End is Really the Beginning

"Look, He is coming with the clouds, and every eye will see Him . . ."
Revelation 1:7, NIV

"Then I saw a new heaven and a new earth.
God had recreated it just as He had made it in the beginning.
The old heaven and earth were gone and so were the vast oceans.

*I, John, saw the holy city, New Jerusalem, come down out of heaven from God,
prepared as a bride beautifully dressed to meet her husband.*

*I heard a loud voice coming from the throne,
saying, 'God will now make His home on earth.
He will personally live with His people and be with them.
They will be part of His royal family, and God will always be their God.
He will wipe away all their tears, and there will be no more death, or sadness,
or crying or pain. The former things are passed away.'"*
Revelation 21:1-4, CW

Dear Heavenly Father, Son, and Holy Spirit,
I love these verses . . . they take my breath away.

Thank You for sharing a vision with Your disciple, John.
This is John's eyewitness account of heaven
so that we would know what to expect and long for.

To think that every eye will see You in all Your glory!
To think that heaven will be absolutely quiet . . .
for the first time, ever.
It will be empty . . .
because all of heaven will be coming to get us!
I get goose bumps . . . just thinking how awesome it will be!

"He who testifies to all these things says it again:

'I'm on My way! I'll be there soon!' "

Your Friend,
Jesus

Revelation 22:20, MSG

The End

Please let me know how this book has touched your life.

You may contact me at:

impossiblejoy@yahoo.com

Love, Gracie

Lightning Source UK Ltd.
Milton Keynes UK
UKHW022020141022
410434UK00009B/523